Learn Blockchain Programming with JavaScript

Build your very own Blockchain and decentralized network with JavaScript and Node.js

Eric Traub

BIRMINGHAM - MUMBAI

Learn Blockchain Programming with JavaScript

Copyright © 2018 Packt Publishing

Commissioning Editor: Kunal Chaudhari
Acquisition Editor: Devanshi Doshi
Content Development Editor: Onkar Wani
Technical Editor: Sachin Sunilkumar
Copy Editor: Safis Editing
Project Coordinator: Kinjal Bari
Proofreader: Safis Editing
Indexer: Priyanka Dhadke
Graphics: Alishon Mendonsa
Production Coordinator: Jyoti Chauhan

First published: November 2018

Production reference: 1291118

Published by Packt Publishing Ltd.
Livery Place
35 Livery Street
Birmingham
B3 2PB, UK.

ISBN 978-1-78961-882-2

www.packtpub.com

`mapt.io`

Mapt is an online digital library that gives you full access to over 5,000 books and videos, as well as industry leading tools to help you plan your personal development and advance your career. For more information, please visit our website.

Why subscribe?

- Spend less time learning and more time coding with practical eBooks and Videos from over 4,000 industry professionals

- Improve your learning with Skill Plans built especially for you

- Get a free eBook or video every month

- Mapt is fully searchable

- Copy and paste, print, and bookmark content

Packt.com

Did you know that Packt offers eBook versions of every book published, with PDF and ePub files available? You can upgrade to the eBook version at `www.packt.com` and as a print book customer, you are entitled to a discount on the eBook copy. Get in touch with us at `customercare@packtpub.com` for more details.

At `www.packt.com`, you can also read a collection of free technical articles, sign up for a range of free newsletters, and receive exclusive discounts and offers on Packt books and eBooks.

Contributors

About the author

Eric Traub currently works as a software engineer in New York City. He has extensive experience working as a teacher and instructing people in a variety of different subjects. He changed his career from teaching to software engineering because of the excitement it brings to him and the passion that he has for it. He is now lucky enough to have the opportunity to combine both of these passions – software engineering and teaching!

> *First of all, I would like to thank Packt Publishing for making this book possible. It has been a great experience working with you to bring this project to life. I would also like to thank everyone who has supported me in this process, including my family and friends. Finally, I want to give a special thanks to my parents, who have shown unconditional love and support for me in everything I do.*

Packt is searching for authors like you

Table of Contents

Preface

With the help of this book, you'll get to build your own blockchain prototype and a decentralized network by using the JavaScript programming language. Building your own blockchain will help you understand various concepts related to blockchains, such as how blockchain technology works under the hood, how decentralized blockchain networks function, and how to code the blockchain and decentralized network using JavaScript. Also, you will get to learn why blockchain is such a secure and valuable technology.

The blockchain that you'll build throughout this book will have functionalities that are similar to those you would find on a real-life blockchain, such as Bitcoin or Ethereum. Your blockchain will have functionalities such as the ability to mine new blocks, create new and immutable transactions, and perform a proof of work to secure the blockchain. In addition to these, your blockchain will consist of many other important features. You'll get to explore those as you read further through the chapters.

When you have completed this book, you will have a thorough understanding of how blockchain technology actually works and why this technology is so secure and valuable. You will also have a deep understanding of how decentralized blockchain networks function and why decentralization is such an important feature for securing the blockchain.

Who this book is for

Learn Blockchain Programming with JavaScript is for JavaScript developers who wish to learn about blockchain programming or build their own blockchain using JavaScript frameworks.

What this book covers

Chapter 1, *Setting Up the Project*, covers what a blockchain actually is and enables readers to understand how it functions. Then, you'll get to learn how to set up a project in order to create your very own blockchain.

Chapter 2, *Building a Blockchain*, covers how to add various functionalities to your blockchain. You will implement the functionalities in the blockchain, creating some amazing methods such as `createNewBlock`, `creatNewTransaction`, and `getLastBlock`. Once these methods are added to the blockchain, you will test them to verify that they are working perfectly. Also, you'll get to learn about the hashing method, that is, SHA256 hashing, and then implement a method to generate a hash for your block data. Also, you'll get to explore what a proof of work is, how it benefits the blockchain, and how to implement it.

Chapter 3, *Accessing the Blockchain through an API*, explains how to set up Express.js in your project, as well as how to use it to build the API/server. Then, you will build various server endpoints for your blockchain and test these endpoints to verify whether or not they are working properly.

Chapter 4, *Creating a Decentralized Blockchain Network*, covers how to set up a decentralized network for your blockchain. In this chapter, you will get to learn a lot of new concepts related to how to set up various nodes and interconnect them to form a network. You'll also define various endpoints, such as `/register-and-broadcast-node`, `/register-node`, and `/register-nodes-bulk`. These endpoints will assist you in implementing the decentralized blockchain network.

Chapter 5, *Synchronizing the Network*, explains how to synchronize the entire decentralized blockchain network so as to have the same transaction data and blocks on all the nodes in the blockchain. You'll implement network synchronization by refactoring the endpoints to broadcast the data to all the nodes present in the network.

Chapter 6, *Consensus Algorithm*, explains how to build your own consensus algorithm, which implements the longest chain rule. Through implementing this algorithm, you will have built a blockchain that is similar to a real-life blockchain.

Chapter 7, *Block Explorer*, explains how to build an amazing user interface to explore the blockchain that you have built over the course of the book.

Chapter 8, *In Conclusion...*, provides a quick summary of everything you will have learned throughout the course of this book. You will also explore what more you can do to improve the blockchain that you have developed.

To get the most out of this book

A basic knowledge of JavaScript is recommended. You will also be required to install Node.js on your system.

The code and implementation of examples in this book were executed on macOS. However, if you want to implement all of these using a Windows PC, you will have to install the necessary requirements for it.

Download the example code files

You can download the example code files for this book from your account at www.packt.com. If you purchased this book elsewhere, you can visit www.packt.com/support and register to have the files emailed directly to you.

You can download the code files by following these steps:

1. Log in or register at www.packt.com.
2. Select the **SUPPORT** tab.
3. Click on **Code Downloads & Errata**.
4. Enter the name of the book in the **Search** box and follow the onscreen instructions.

Once the file is downloaded, please make sure that you unzip or extract the folder using the latest version of:

- WinRAR/7-Zip for Windows
- Zipeg/iZip/UnRarX for Mac
- 7-Zip/PeaZip for Linux

The code bundle for the book is also hosted on GitHub at https://github.com/PacktPublishing/Learn-Blockchain-Programming-with-JavaScript. In case there's an update to the code, it will be updated on the existing GitHub repository.

We also have other code bundles from our rich catalog of books and videos available at https://github.com/PacktPublishing/. Check them out!

Conventions used

There are a number of text conventions used throughout this book.

CodeInText: Indicates code words in text, database table names, folder names, filenames, file extensions, pathnames, dummy URLs, user input, and Twitter handles. Here is an example: "Mount the downloaded WebStorm-10*.dmg disk image file as another disk in your system."

A block of code is set as follows:

```
Blockchain.prototype.createNewBlock = function () {

}
```

When we wish to draw your attention to a particular part of a code block, the relevant lines or items are set in bold:

```
Blockchain.prototype.createNewBlock = function (nonce, previousBlockHash, hash) {

}
```

Any command-line input or output is written as follows:

```
cd dev
touch blockchain.js  test.js
```

Bold: Indicates a new term, an important word, or words that you see on screen. For example, words in menus or dialog boxes appear in the text like this. Here is an example: "Go to **More Tools,** and then select the **Developer Tools** option."

 Warnings or important notes appear like this.

 Tips and tricks appear like this.

Get in touch

Feedback from our readers is always welcome.

General feedback: If you have questions about any aspect of this book, mention the book title in the subject of your message and email us at customercare@packtpub.com.

Errata: Although we have taken every care to ensure the accuracy of our content, mistakes do happen. If you have found a mistake in this book, we would be grateful if you would report this to us. Please visit www.packt.com/submit-errata, selecting your book, clicking on the Errata Submission Form link, and entering the details.

Piracy: If you come across any illegal copies of our works in any form on the internet, we would be grateful if you would provide us with the location address or website name. Please contact us at copyright@packt.com with a link to the material.

If you are interested in becoming an author: If there is a topic that you have expertise in, and you are interested in either writing or contributing to a book, please visit authors.packtpub.com.

Reviews

Please leave a review. Once you have read and used this book, why not leave a review on the site that you purchased it from? Potential readers can then see and use your unbiased opinion to make purchase decisions, we at Packt can understand what you think about our products, and our authors can see your feedback on their book. Thank you!

For more information about Packt, please visit packt.com.

Setting up the Project

Welcome to *Learning Blockchain Programming with JavaScript*. As the name suggests, in this book, you'll learn how to build a fully functional blockchain from scratch using the JavaScript programming language. The blockchain that you build will have functionalities that are similar to those you would find in a production-level blockchain for examples such as Bitcoin or Ethereum.

In this book, you will understand how blockchain technology actually workes by learning to build your own blockchain and understanding the decentralized network. Toward the conclusion of the book, you will have a full-fledged blockchain prototype that is hosted on a decentralized network, and you'll have gained a great deal of knowledge and understanding as to how blockchains actually work under the hood.

The blockchain that we will create throughout this book will be able to carry out the following functionalities:

- Perform a proof of work to secure the blockchain
- Create new blocks through a mining process
- Create new, immutable transactions
- Validate the entire blockchain and all of the data within each block
- Retrieve address/transaction/block data

Along with these, the blockchain will have many other important features. You'll get to explore those as you read further through the chapters.

To follow this book, all you'll need is a computer and some basic knowledge of the JavaScript programming language.

Firstly, in this introductory chapter, let's try to understand what blockchain actually is. This will help you to become familiar with the concept of blockchain, as this is a prerequisite for the book. Then we'll move on to learn how to set up the project to create our own blockchain.

So, let's get started!

What is a blockchain?

In this section, let's go through a brief explanation of what a blockchain is. Simply put, a **blockchain** is an immutable, distributed ledger. Now, these words may seem quite complex, but when we try to break them down, it is very easy to understand them. Let's begin by exploring what a ledger actually is. A ledger is simply a collection of financial accounts or transactions (or in other words, a record of transactions that people have made).

Let's take a look at the following example to get a better understanding of ledgers. In this example, Kim paid Joe $30 and Kevin paid Jen $80. A ledger is simply a document that is used to keep track of these transactions. You can see this depicted in the following screenshot:

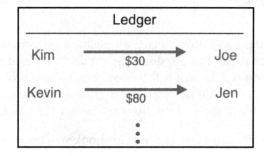

Now, what does it mean for a blockchain to be immutable? This means that it cannot be changed—ever. Consequently, when a transaction is recorded, it cannot be undone. Other factors that cannot be changed include the amount of money that was sent or the people who took part in the transaction. Once a transaction is made, no aspects of that transaction can be changed because it is immutable.

In the world today, we see many applications, platforms, and networks that are all centralized. Take Facebook, for example. Everyone who uses Facebook has to trust this company is protecting their data and not abusing it. Compared to this, blockchain is different. Blockchain technology is not centralized like Facebook, Google, or most other entities. Instead, it is a distributed network, which means that any given blockchain network is not controlled by a single entity, but is run by normal, everyday people. Blockchains, such as Bitcoin, are supported and hosted by thousands of people worldwide. Consequently, all of our data, or the ledger in this case, is not at the mercy of a single company or entity. This proves to be a great benefit of blockchain technology because by being distributed, we do not have to trust a single company with our data. Instead, our data is persisted by the entire network of thousands of different people who are all acting independently.

Each individual who contributes to the blockchain network is called a node, and each node has the exact same copy of the ledger. Therefore, the ledger data is hosted and synchronized across the entire network.

So, a blockchain is an immutable distributed ledger. This means that it is a ledger in which the transactions can never be changed and the blockchain itself is distributed across the network and run by thousands of independent people, groups, or nodes.

The blockchain is a very powerful technology which is still in its infancy, but its future is very exciting. There are many ways that blockchain technology can be applied to our world today to make certain industries more secure, efficient, and trustworthy. Some industries that could be transformed with the help of blockchain technology include financial services, healthcare, credit, governments, energy industries, and many others. Pretty much every industry out there could benefit from a more secure, distributed form of data management. You can observe that blockchain technology is at a very exciting stage right now, and many people are excited about what the future holds for it.

Now that we're aware of what blockchain is, let's move onto setting up our project environment to build our blockchain.

What you will learn...

This book will help you to gain a deeper understanding of blockchain technology by building your own blockchain from scratch. Blockchain is a fairly new technology, and while it can seem tough and slightly overwhelming to learn at first, we're going to take a step-by-step approach and break it down in order to understand how it works under the hood. By the time you finish this book, you will have a very solid understanding of how blockchain technology works, and you will have built your own entire blockchain as well.

In this book, we will start by building the blockchain itself. At this point, we will build a blockchain data structure that has the following abilities:

- Proofing work
- Mining new blocks
- Creating transactions
- Validating the chain
- Retrieving address data and other functionalities

Thereafter, we will create an API or a server that will allow us to interact with our blockchain from the internet. Through our API, we will be able to use all of the functionality that we have built into our blockchain data structure.

Furthermore, you'll be learning to create a decentralized network. This means that we'll have multiple servers running and acting as separate nodes. We'll also make sure that all of the nodes interact with each other properly and share data with each other in the correct format. In addition, you'll learn how to synchronize the entire network by making sure that any new nodes or transactions that are created are broadcast throughout the entire network.

We'll then move onto creating a consensus algorithm. This algorithm will be used to make sure that our entire blockchain stays synchronized and that this algorithm will be used to make sure that each node in our network has the correct blockchain data.

Finally, we will create a block explorer. This will be a user interface that will allow us to explore our blockchain in a user-friendly manner, and it will also allow us to query our blockchain for specific block transactions and addresses.

Firstly, however, we need to set up our development environment.

Environment setup

Let's get started with building our blockchain project. The first thing we're going to do is open our terminal and create our blockchain directory by typing commands into the terminal, as seen in the following screenshot:

Let's begin by creating a folder called `programs`. Inside this folder, let's create a directory called `blockchain`. This directory is currently empty. Inside of this `blockchain` directory is where we're going to be doing all of our programming. We are going to be building our entire blockchain inside of this `blockchain` directory.

Now our `blockchain` directory is ready, and the first thing that we need to do is to add some folders and files into it. The first folder that we want to put into the directory will be called `dev`, so we want to make sure that we are inside of the `blockchain` directory, and then let's type the following command into the terminal:

```
mkdir dev
```

Inside this `dev` directory is where we are going to be doing most of our coding. This is where we're going to build our blockchain data structure and create our API to interact with our blockchain, test it, and fulfill other similar tasks. Next, inside this `dev` folder, let's create two files: `blockchain.js` and `test.js`. To do this, enter the following command:

```
cd dev
touch blockchain.js test.js
```

The `touch` term in the preceding command line will help us in creating the mentioned files. The `blockchain.js` file is where we will type our code to create the blockchain and the `test.js` file is where we will write code to test our blockchain.

Next, let's return back to our `blockchain` directory by typing the following command in the terminal:

```
cd ..
```

In the `blockchain` directory, let's run the following command to create the npm project:

```
npm init
```

After running the preceding command, you will get some options on your terminal. To set up the project, you can just press *Enter* through those options.

So, this is pretty much all we need to do in order to set up our project folder structure. Now, if you go to our `blockchain` directory and open it with a text editor such as Sublime or Atom (or whatever you would like), you will get to see the file structure, as seen in the following screenshot:

The `blockchain` directory consists of the `dev` folder that we just created. Inside the `dev` folder, we can observe our `blockchain.js` and `test.js` files. Also, when we run the `npm init` command, it creates the `package.json` file for us. This `.json` file will keep track of our project and any dependencies that we need, allowing us to run scripts. We'll be working more inside of this `package.json` file in further chapters, so you'll become more familiar with it as we progress through the book.

Project source code

Before we start coding our blockchain, it is worth noting that the entire source code for this book can be found on GitHub at the following link: `https://github.com/PacktPublishing/Learn-Blockchain-Programming-with-JavaScript`. In this repository, you'll find the completed code for the entire project, and you will also be able to explore all of the files that we will be building in further chapters. Therefore, this may be a good resource for you to use as you make your way through the book.

Summary

To summarize this introductory chapter, we began by exploring what a blockchain actually is and understanding how it functions. Then we moved onto setting up our project to create our very own blockchain. We also had a quick overview of all of the topics you'll get to learn about in this book.

In the next chapter, we'll build our blockchain by learning about the constructor function, prototype object, block method, transaction method, and many more important concepts.

2
Building a Blockchain

In the previous chapter, we learned about what a blockchain is and how it functions. In addition, we learned how to set up a project to build our blockchain. In this chapter, you will begin building the blockchain and all of its functionalities. First, let's create the blockchain data structure using a constructor function, and then we'll add a lot of different types of functionalities to our blockchain by adding different methods to its prototype.

We're then going to give the blockchain certain functionalities, such as creating new blocks and transactions, as well as the ability to hash data and blocks. We'll also give it the ability to do a proof of work and many other functionalities that a blockchain should be able to do. We'll then make sure that the blockchain is fully functional by testing the added functionalities as we progress.

By building each piece of the blockchain step by step, you will gain a better understanding of how blockchain actually works under the hood. You may also realize that once you dive into it, creating a blockchain is not as complicated as it sounds.

In this chapter, we'll cover the following topics:

- Learning how to create a Blockchain constructor function
- Building and testing various methods such as `createNewBlock`, `createNewTransaction`, and `hashBlock` to add functionalities to the blockchain
- Understanding what proof of work is and learning how to implement it for our blockchain
- Creating and testing a genesis block

So, let's get started!

Before we get building...

Before we get into building the blockchain, there are two crucial concepts that we need to familiarize ourselves with. These important concepts are as follows:

- The JavaScript constructor function
- The prototype object

An explanation of the JavaScript constructor function

Becoming familiar with the constructor function is important as we'll be using it to build our blockchain data structure. By now, you must be wondering what a constructor function is and what it actually does.

A constructor function is simply a function that creates an object class and allows you to easily create multiple instances of that particular class. What this actually means is that the constructor function allows you to create a lot of objects very quickly. All of these objects that are created will have the same properties and functionalities because they are all part of the same class. Now, all of this might seem a little bit confusing when you hear it for the first time, but don't worry — we'll try to understand what a constructor function is with the help of an example.

Let's take Facebook, for example. Facebook has over one-and-a half billion users, which are all objects of the same class and have similar properties such as name, email, password, birthday, and so on. For our example, let's assume that we are building the Facebook website and want to create a bunch of different users for it. Let's do this by creating a `User` constructor function.

To learn and explore the constructor functions, let's use the Google Chrome console. We can access the console by going to Google Chrome and simply pressing *command + option + J* for Mac users and *Ctrl + Shift + I* for Windows users. Alternatively, we can simply go to the menu option, go to **More Tools,** and then select the **Developer Tools** option, as shown in the following screenshot:

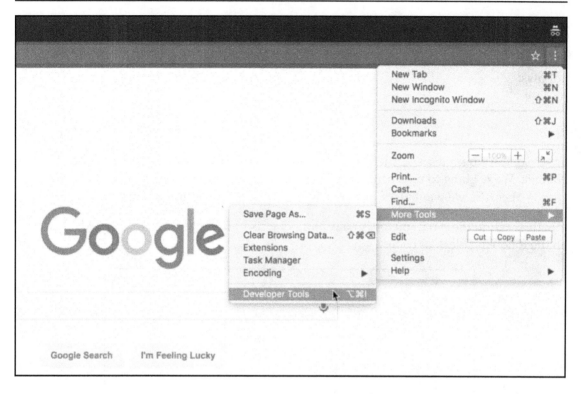

Following the aforementioned steps will open the console for you, as shown in the following screenshot:

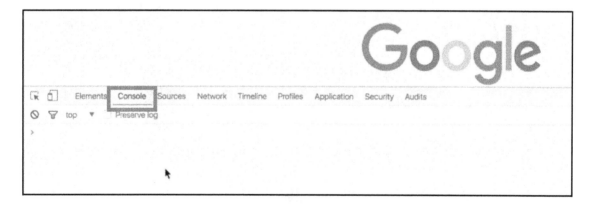

The constructor function that we'll be coding in this example will allow us to create multiple users or multiple user objects that will have the same properties and functionalities. The code to create this `User` constructor function begins by defining it as follows:

```
function User() {

}
```

Inside of the parentheses, `()`, let's pass the properties that we want each of our `User` objects to have. We're going to pass properties such as `firstName`, `lastName`, `age`, and `gender` because we want all of our user objects to have these components.

We then assign these parameters to our `User` objects by using the `this` keyword, as shown in the following block of code:

```
Elements   Console   Sources   Network   Timeline

     top  ▼   ◯ Preserve log

> function User(firstName, lastName, age, gender) {
      this.firstName = firstName;
      this.lastName = lastName;
      this.age = age;
      this.gender = gender;
  }
```

This is how we define the constructor function in JavaScript. Now, reading through the preceding code block, you might be wondering what we did and what the `this` keyword is all about.

We're going to use this constructor function to create a lot of user objects. The `this` keyword is simply referring to each of the user objects that we're going to create. This might all seem a bit overwhelming right now, but let's run through a couple of examples and try to gain more clarity on it.

Let's begin using our `User` constructor function. To make some `User` objects, also known as `User` instances, follow these steps:

1. The first user that we are going to create – let's call it `user1` – will be defined as follows:

   ```
   var user1 = new User('John','Smith',26,'male');
   ```

In the preceding code, you may have noticed that we used the new keyword to invoke our constructor function and make a user object, which is how we get our constructor function to work.

2. Then press *Enter,* and user1 is in the system. Now, if we type user1 in the console, we'll be able to see what we just created in the previous step:

```
> user1
< ▼ User {firstName: "John", lastName: "Smith", age: 26, gender: "male"}
```

In the preceding output screenshot, we can see that user1 is an object of the User class. We can also see that user1 has a firstName of John, a lastName of Smith, an age of 26, and gender of male because these are the parameters that we passed into the constructor function.

3. For clarity, try adding one more user. This time, we'll create another user called user200 and pass in into the new User ( ) function with the user's properties, such as a first name of Jill, a last name of Robinson, an age of 25, and a female gender:

```
var user200 = new User('Jill', 'Robinson', 25, 'female');
```

4. By pressing *Enter,* our new user200 will be in the system. Now, if we type user200 into the console and press *Enter,* we'll see the following output:

```
> user200
< ▼ User {firstName: "Jill", lastName: "Robinson", age: 25, gender: "female"}
```

In the preceding output, we can see that user200 is an object of the User class, just like user1, and that she has a first name of Jill, a last name of Robinson, an age of 25, and a female gender because these were the parameters that we passed into our constructor function.

Now, you might be wondering how all of these properties that we mentioned got assigned correctly. This was all due to the this keyword that we mentioned earlier. When we create our constructor function, we use the this keyword to assign properties. When it comes to a constructor function, the this keyword does not refer to the function that it is in – in our case, the User function. Instead, this refers to the object that will be created by the constructor function.

This signifies that if we use the constructor function to create an object, we must make sure that the property and their objects are first name, last name, age, and gender, or whenever you make your constructor function, set the `firstName` property as equal to the `firstName` parameter that is passed in, and do the same for the rest of the properties.

This is how a constructor function works and how the `this` keyword plays an important role in the constructor function.

Explanation of the prototype object

Another important concept that we need to discuss before getting into coding our blockchain data structure is the prototype object. The **prototype object** is simply an object that multiple other objects can refer to in order to get any information or functionality that they need. For our example, which we discussed in the previous section, each of our constructor functions will have a prototype that all of their instances will be able to refer to. Let's try to understand what a prototype object means by exploring a couple of examples.

For example, if we take our `User` constructor function that we created in the previous section, we can put those properties onto its prototype. Then, all of our user instances like `user1` and `user200` will have access to and be able to use that prototype. Let's add a property on our `User` prototype and see what happens. To add a property on the user prototype, we will type the following code:

```
User.prototype.
```

Then let's add the name of the property to the preceding code. For example, let's say we want a property email domain:

```
User.prototype.emailDomain
```

For our example, assume that Facebook wants every user to have an `@facebook.com` email address, so we'll set the email domain property as follows:

```
User.prototype.emailDomain = '@facebook.com';
```

Now let's check out our `user1` object again:

```
> User.prototype.emailDomain = '@facebook.com';
< "@facebook.com"
> user1
< ▼ User {firstName: "John", lastName: "Smith", age: 26, gender: "male"}
```

In the preceding screenshot, we can see that `user1` does not have the email domain property that we just added to it. However, we can expand the `user1` object, as well as its dunder proto, as highlighted in the following screenshot:

```
‹  ▼User {firstName: "John", lastName: "Smith", age: 26, gender: "male"}
      age: 26
      firstName: "John"
      gender: "male"
      lastName: "Smith"
    ▼__proto__:
        emailDomain: "@facebook.com"
      ▶constructor: f User(firstName, lastName, age, gender)
      ▶__proto__: Object
```

When we do this, we can observe the `emailDomain` property that we just added, which is set to `@facebook.com`.

Just to clarify, the dunder proto and the prototype object that we actually put the `emailDomain` property on are actually not exactly the same, but are very similar. Basically, anything that we put on the constructor function prototype will have access to the dunder proto of any of the objects that we create with the constructor function.

So, if we put `emailDomain` on the constructor function prototype, we'll have access to it on the `user1` dunder proto, the `user200` dunder proto, and the dunder protos of any other user instance that we've created.

Now let's get back to the `emailDomain` property. We put the `emailDomain` property and the user prototype. We can see that we don't have the property on the actual `user200` object, but we have that property under the `user200` dunder proto. So, if we type the following command, we will still have access to that property:

```
user200.emailDomain
```

We should then see the following output:

```
>  user200.emailDomain
‹  "@facebook.com"
```

So, this is how the prototype object works. If we put a property on the constructor function's prototype, all of the instances of the constructor function will have access to that property.

The same thing applies for any methods or functions that we might want all of our instances to have. Let's take a look at another example, assuming that we want all of our user instances to have a `getEmailAddress` method. We can put this on the prototype of the constructor function as follows:

```
User.prototype.getEmailAddress = function () {
}
```

Now let's have this `getEmailAddress` method return some specific properties, as follows (highlighted):

```
User.prototype.getEmailAddress = function () {
    return this.firstName + this.lastName + this.emailDomain;
}
```

Now both `user1` and `user200` should have this method under their dunder proto, so let's check it out. Type in our users, and under their dunder proto you will get to observe the preceding function, as shown in the following screenshot:

```
> user1
< ▼ User {firstName: "John", lastName: "Smith", age: 26, gender: "male"}
      age: 26
      firstName: "John"
      gender: "male"
      lastName: "Smith"
    ▼ __proto__:
        emailDomain: "@facebook.com"
      ▶ getEmailAddress: f ()
      ▶ constructor: f User(firstName, lastName, age, gender)
      ▶ __proto__: Object
> user200
< ▼ User {firstName: "Jill", lastName: "Robinson", age: 25, gender: "female"}
      age: 25
      firstName: "Jill"
      gender: "female"
      lastName: "Robinson"
    ▼ __proto__:
        emailDomain: "@facebook.com"
      ▶ getEmailAddress: f ()
      ▶ constructor: f User(firstName, lastName, age, gender)
      ▶ __proto__: Object
```

In the preceding screenshot, we can observe that both `user1` and `user200` have the `getEmailAddress` method under their dunder proto.

Now, if we type `user200.getEmailAddress` and then invoke it, the method will then create user200's Facebook email address for us, as shown in the following screenshot:

```
> user200.getEmailAddress();
< "JillRobinson@facebook.com"
```

A similar thing will happen if we invoke the method for `user1`:

```
> user1.getEmailAddress();
< "JohnSmith@facebook.com"
```

So, this is how we use the prototype object with a constructor function. If we want our constructor function instances to all have the properties that are the same for all of them, or all have a method that is the same for all of them, we will put it on the prototype instead of the constructor function itself. This will help in keeping the instances more lean and cleaner.

This is all the background information that we need to know in order to start coding our blockchain data structure. In the following section, we will start building our blockchain by using a constructor function and the prototype object.

Blockchain constructor function

Let's get started with building our blockchain data structure. We'll start by opening all of the files that we have in our blockchain directory by using the Sublime editor. If you are comfortable using any other editor, you can use that too. Open our entire blockchain directory in whichever editor you prefer.

We'll be building our entire blockchain data structure in the `dev/blockchain.js` file that we created in Chapter 1, *Setting up the Project*. Let's build this blockchain data structure by using a constructor function that we learned about in the previous section. So, let's begin:

For the constructor by type the following:

```
function Blockchain () {
}
```

For now, the `Blockchain ()` function is not going to take any parameters.

Next, inside of our constructor function, we are going to add the following terms:

```
function Blockchain () {
    this.chain = [];
    this.newTransactions = [];
}
```

In the preceding code block, `[]` defines an array, and the `this.chain = [];` is where the meat of our blockchain will be stored. All of the blocks that we mine will be stored in this particular array as a chain, while `this.newTransactions = [];` is where we will hold all of the new transactions that are created before they are placed into a block.

All of this might seem a little bit confusing and overwhelming right now, but don't worry about it. Let's dive deeper into this in future sections.

When defining the preceding function, we have initiated the process of creating the blockchain data structure. Now, you might be wondering why we are using a constructor function to build our blockchain data structure instead of a class; the answer to this is that this is simply a preference. We prefer to create constructor functions over classes in JavaScript because in JavaScript there really are no classes. Classes in JavaScript are simply a kind of a sugar coating on top of constructor functions and the object prototype. So, we simply prefer to just stick with constructor functions.

However, if you want to create a blockchain by using a class, you could do something such as in the following block of code:

```
class Blockchain {
    constructor() {
        this.chain = [];
        this.newTransactions = [];
    }

    // Here you can build out all of the methods
    // that we are going to write inside of this
    // Blockchain class.

}
```

So, either way, if you prefer using a constructor function or using a class, it would work just fine.

This is it – with defining our function, we've began the process of building our blockchain data structure. In further sections, we'll continue to build on this.

Building the createNewBlock method

Let's continue with building our blockchain data structure. After defining our constructor function in the previous section, the next thing that we want to do with our constructor function is to place a method in our `Blockchain` function. This method that we are going to create will be called `createNewBlock`. As its name suggests, this method will create a new block for us. Let's follow the below mentioned steps to build the method:

1. The `createNewBlock` method will be defined as follows:

   ```
   Blockchain.prototype.createNewBlock = function () {

   }
   ```

2. Now we've got this `createNewBlock` method on our blockchain `prototype` object. This method will take the three parameters, as highlighted in the following line of code:

   ```
   Blockchain.prototype.createNewBlock = function (nonce,
   previousBlockHash, hash) {

   }
   ```

   We'll learn in depth about these three parameters in further sections, so don't worry if you're not familiar with them.

3. Now, the next thing that we want to do inside of our `createNewBlock` method is to create a `newBlock` object. Let's define this as follows:

   ```
   Blockchain.prototype.createNewBlock = function (nonce,
   previousBlockHash, hash) {
       const newBlock = {
       };

   }
   ```

   This `newBlock` object is going to be a new block inside of our `BlockChain`, so all of the data is going to be stored inside of this block. This `newBlock` object is a pretty important part of our blockchain.

4. Next, on the `newBlock` object, we're going to have an `index` property. This `index` value will basically be the block number. It will describe what number of block the `newBlock` is in our chain (for example, it may be the first block):

```
Blockchain.prototype.createNewBlock = function (nonce,
previousBlockHash, hash) {
    const newBlock = {
        index: this.chain.length + 1,
    };

}
```

5. Our next property is going to be a `timestamp`, because we want to know when the block was created:

```
Blockchain.prototype.createNewBlock = function (nonce,
previousBlockHash, hash) {
    const newBlock = {
        index: this.chain.length + 1,
        timestamp: Date.now(),
    };

}
```

6. Then, the next property we will add will be for the `transactions`. When we create a new block, we'll want to put all of the new transactions or the pending transactions that have just been created into the new block so that they're inside of our blockchain and can never be changed:

```
Blockchain.prototype.createNewBlock = function (nonce,
previousBlockHash, hash) {
    const newBlock = {
        index: this.chain.length + 1,
        timestamp: Date.now(),
        transactions: this.newTransactions,
    };

}
```

The preceding highlighted line of code states that all of the transactions in the block should be the new transactions that are waiting to be placed into a block.

7. The next property that we are going to have on our block is a `nonce`, and this will be equal to the `nonce` parameter that we passed into our function earlier:

```
Blockchain.prototype.createNewBlock = function (nonce,
previousBlockHash, hash) {
```

```
const newBlock = {
    index: this.chain.length + 1,
    timestamp: Date.now(),
    transactions: this.newTransactions,
    nonce: nonce,
};

}
```

Now, you might be wondering what a `nonce` is. Basically, a nonce comes from a proof of work. In our case, this is simply any number; it doesn't matter which. This nonce is pretty much proof that we've created this new block in a legitimate way by using a `proofOfWork` method.

All of this might seem a little bit confusing right now, but don't worry — once we build more on our blockchain data structure, it will be much easier to understand how everything works together to create a functional blockchain. So, if you don't understand what a nonce is right now, don't worry about it. We're going to deal with this property in further sections, and it will become clearer as we move on.

8. The next property is going to be a `hash`:

```
Blockchain.prototype.createNewBlock = function (nonce,
previousBlockHash, hash) {
    const newBlock = {
        index: this.chain.length + 1,
        timestamp: Date.now(),
        transactions: this.newTransactions,
        nonce: nonce,
        hash: hash,
    };

}
```

Basically, this `hash` will be the data from our `newBlock`. What's going to happen is we're going to pass our transactions or our `newTransactions` into a hashing function. What this means is that all of our transactions are going to be compressed into a single string of code, which will be our `hash`.

9. Finally, our last property on our `newBlock` will be our `previousBlockHash`:

```
Blockchain.prototype.createNewBlock = function (nonce,
previousBlockHash, hash) {
    const newBlock = {
        index: this.chain.length + 1,
```

```
        timestamp: Date.now(),
        transactions: this.newTransactions,
        nonce: nonce,
        hash: hash,
        previousBlockHash: previousBlockHash,
    };


}
```

This `previousBlockHash` property is very similar to our `hash` property, except our `hash` property deals with the data from our current block hashed into a string, and the `previousBlockHash` property deals with the data from our previous block or the previous block to the current block hashed into a string.

So, `hash` and `previousBlockHash` are both hashes. The only difference is that the `hash` property deals with the data of the current block, and, the `previousBlockHash` property deals with the hashing of the data of the previous block. This is how you create a new block, and this is what every block in our blockchain will look like.

10. Continuing with our `createNewBlock` method, the next thing that we want to do is set `this.newTransaction` as equal to an empty array, as follows:

```
Blockchain.prototype.createNewBlock = function (nonce,
previousBlockHash, hash) {
    const newBlock = {
        index: this.chain.length + 1,
        timestamp: Date.now(),
        transactions: this.newTransactions,
        nonce: nonce,
        hash: hash,
        previousBlockHash: previousBlockHash,
    };
    this.newTransaction = [];


}
```

We do this because, once we create our new block, we are putting all of the new transactions into the `newBlock`. Therefore, we want to clear out the entire new transactions array so that we can start over for the next block.

11. Next, what we simply want to do is take the new block that we've created and push it into our chain, and then we're going to return the `newBlock`:

```
Blockchain.prototype.createNewBlock = function (nonce,
previousBlockHash, hash) {
```

```
const newBlock = {
    index: this.chain.length + 1,
    timestamp: Date.now(),
    transactions: this.newTransaction,
    nonce: nonce,
    hash: hash,
    previousBlockHash: previousBlockHash,
};
this.newTransaction = [];
this.chain.push(newBlock);
return newBlock;
}
```

By adding these last two lines of code, our createNewBlock method is ready. Basically, what this method does on a high level is it creates a new block. Inside of this block, we have our transactions and the new transactions that have been created since our last block was mined. After we've created a new block, let's clear out the new transactions, push the new block into our chain, and simply return our new block.

Testing the createNewBlock method

Now lets test the createNewBlock method that we created in the preceding section:

1. The first thing that we need to do is export our Blockchain constructor function because we are going to use this function in our test.js file. So, to export the constructor function, we will go to the bottom of the blockchain.js file, type the following line of code, and then save the file:

```
module.exports = Blockchain;
```

2. Next, go to the dev/test.js file, as this is where we will be testing our createNewBlock method. Now, the first thing that we want to do in our dev/test.js file is import our Blockchain constructor function, so type the following:

```
const Blockchain = require('./blockchain');
```

This preceding line of code simply requires or calls the blockchain.js file.

Testing the Blockchain constructor function

Let's test the Blockchain constructor function as follows:

1. Lets make an instance of our `Blockchain` constructor function, so we will add the following line of code:

   ```
   const bitcoin = new Blockchain();
   ```

2. The `bitcoin` variable in the preceding line of code is just used for the purpose of an example. Then we add the following line of code:

   ```
   console.log(bitcoin);
   ```

   With the preceding line of code, `bitcoin` should be our blockchain. There is currently no data or blocks in this, but it should log out as a blockchain. Let's save the `test.js` file and run the test to observe the output on the terminal window.

3. Now go to our terminal window. In here, we're currently in the `blockchain` directory, and our `test.js` file is in our `dev` folder, so type the following command in the terminal:

   ```
   node dev/test.js
   ```

   This preceding line of code will allow us to run the test that we have written to test our `Blockchain` constructor function.

4. Now press *Enter*, and we'll get to observe the `Blockchain` on the terminal window, as highlighted in the following screenshot:

```
                            1. Eric@Erics-MBP-2: ~/programs/blockchain (zsh)
→  blockchain ls
dev            package.json
→  blockchain node dev/test.js
Blockchain { chain: [], newTransactions: [] }
```

From the output in the preceding screenshot, we can observe that `Blockchain` has an empty chain and an empty transactions array. This is exactly what we expected the output to be.

Testing the createNewBlock method

Let's follow the below mentioned steps to test the createNewBlock method:

1. Firstly, underneath where we created our `bitcoin` variable, type in the following highlighted line of code:

```
const Blockchain = require('./blockchain');

const bitcoin = new Blockchain();

bitcoin.createNewBlock();

console.log(bitcoin);
```

2. This `createNewBlock()` method requires three parameters, such as `nonce`, `previousBlockHash`, and a `hash`. For test purposes, we can just pass in whatever we want for now. Here, the nonce will just be a number. Then we will create a dummy hash for our `previousBlockHash`, followed by another hash for our `hash` parameter, as follows:

```
bitcoin.createNewBlock(2389,'OIUOEREDHKHKD','78s97d4x6dsf');
```

Right now, we are creating our `bitcoin` blockchain, followed by a new block in our bitcoin blockchain. When we log out of our bitcoin blockchain, we should have one block in it.

3. Save this file and run our `test.js` file again in the terminal. You'll then get to observe the following output:

```
Blockchain {
  chain:
   [ { index: 1,
       timestamp: 1523996453762,
       transactions: [],
       nonce: 2389,
       hash: '90ANSD9F0N9009N',
       previousBlockHash: 'OINA90SDNF90N' } ],
  newTransactions: [] }
```

In the preceding screenshot, you can observe the entire blockchain data structure in the `chain` array. This has one block in it, or one object in it. This block also has the `hash`, `nonce`, and `previousBlockHash` parameters that we had passed. It also has the `timestamp` and the `index` of 1. It has no transactions because we haven't created any transactions yet. Consequently, we can conclude that the `createNewBlock` method works just fine.

4. Now let's test our method even further by creating a couple more blocks in our chain. Let's duplicate the following lines of code multiple times and then try to change the values in it as we wish:

```
bitcoin.createNewBlock(2389,'OIUOEREDHKHKD','78s97d4x6dsf');
```

5. After duplicating the code and changing the value, save the file. Now, when we run our `test.js` file, we should have three blocks in our chain, as shown in the following screenshot:

```
→ blockchain node dev/test.js
Blockchain {
  chain:
   [ { index: 1,
       timestamp: 1523996545066,
       transactions: [],
       nonce: 2389,
       hash: '90ANSD9F0N9009N',
       previousBlockHash: 'OINA90SDNF90N' },
     { index: 2,
       timestamp: 1523996545066,
       transactions: [],
       nonce: 111,
       hash: 'NJNASDNF09ASDF',
       previousBlockHash: 'OIANSDF0AN09' },
     { index: 3,
       timestamp: 1523996545066,
       transactions: [],
       nonce: 2899,
       hash: '99889HBAIUSBDF',
       previousBlockHash: 'UINIUN90ANSDF' } ],
  newTransactions: [] }
```

In the preceding screenshot, you may have observed the three blocks inside of the `chain` array. These are all of the blocks that we've created with our `createNewBlock` method.

Building the getLastBlock method

Now, the next method that we are going to add to our `Blockchain` constructor function will be the `getLastBlock`. This method will simply return the last block in our blockchain to us. Follow the below mentioned steps to build the method:

1. Go to our `dev/blockchain.js` file, and after our `createNewBlock` method, add the following:

   ```
   Blockchain.prototype.getLastBlock = function () {

   }
   ```

2. Inside of this `getLastBlock` method, we will type the following highlighted line of code:

   ```
   Blockchain.prototype.getLastBlock = function () {
       return this.chain[this.chain.length - 1];

   }
   ```

The `[this.chain.length - 1];` in this preceding code defines the position of the block in the chain, which, in our case, is the previous block, therefore negated by `1`. This method is simple and straightforward, and we'll use it in later chapters.

Creating the createNewTransaction method

The next method that we are going to add to our blockchain constructor function is called `createNewTransaction`. This method will create a new transaction for us. Let's follow the below mentioned steps to create the method:

1. Start building up this method by adding the following line of code after our `getLastBlock` method:

   ```
   Blockchain.prototype.createNewTransaction = function () {

   }
   ```

2. The `function ()` will take three parameters, such as the following:

   ```
   Blockchain.prototype.createNewTransaction = function (amount,
   sender, recipient) {

   }
   ```

What these three parameters will do is as follows:

- `amount`: This parameter will take in the amount of the transaction or how much is being sent in this transaction.
- `sender`: This will take in the sender's address.
- `recipient`: This will take in the recipient's address.

3. The next thing that we want to do inside of our `createNewTransaction` method is create a transaction object. So, add the following line of code to our method:

```
const newTransaction = {

}
```

4. This object will have three properties in it. It will have an `amount`, a `sender`, and the `recipient`. These are the same three parameters that we passed into our `function()`. So, type in the following:

```
Blockchain.prototype.createNewTransaction = function (amount,
sender, recipient) {
    const newTransaction = {
        amount: amount,
        sender: sender,
        recipient: recipient,
    };

}
```

This is what our transaction object will look like. All of the transactions that we record on our `Blockchain` are going to look just like this. They all are going to have an amount, a sender, and the recipient, which is pretty straightforward and simple.

5. The next thing that we want to do now is push this `newTransaction` data into our `newTransactions` array. Let's do this by adding the following code after our `newTransaction` object:

```
this.newTransactions.push(newTransaction);
```

So, the new transaction that we just created will now be pushed into our `newTransactions` array.

Now, let's just try to understand what this `newTransactions` array actually is. Basically, what is happening here with this `newTransactions` array is that on our blockchain there are going to be a lot of people who will be making a lot of different transactions. They will be sending money from one person to another and this will be happening repetitively. Every time a new transaction is created, it's going to be pushed into our `newTransactions` array.

However, all of the transactions in this array are not really set in stone. They're not really recorded in our blockchain yet. They will get recorded in our blockchain when a new block is mined, which is when a new block is created. All of these new transactions are pretty much just pending transactions, and they have not been validated yet. They get validated, set in stone, and recorded in our blockchain when we create a new block with the help of the `createNewBlock` method.

In our `createNewBlock` method, you can observe in `transactions:` `this.newTransactions` that we set the transactions on a new block equal to the `newTransactions` or the pending transactions in our blockchain. You can think of this `newTransactions` property on our blockchain as a pending transactions property.

For easy reference, let's actually change all of the `newTransactions` properties in our code to `pendingTransactions` properties. Overall, when a new transaction is created, it is pushed into our `pendingTransactions` array. Then, when a new block is mined or when a new block is created, that's when all of our pending transactions become recorded on our blockchain, and they are then set in stone and can never be changed.

The point of all this is that before our method ends, we want to return in which block we will be able to find the new transaction because our new transaction will be in the next block when it is mined. Consequently, we'll simply type the following code:

```
this.newTransactions.push(newTransaction);
return.this.getlastBlock()['index'] + 1;
```

In the preceding code, `this.getlastBlock()` returns a block object for us. We want to get the index property of this block – adding `['index']` will provide us with the index of the last block in our chain, and adding `+ 1` will provide us with the number of the block our transaction was pushed to.

Let's have a quick recap, the `createNewTransaction` method simply creates a `newTransaction` object, and then we push that `newTransaction` into our `pendingTransactions` array. Finally, we return the number of the block that the `newTransaction` will be added to.

Testing the createNewTransaction method

Let's test the `createNewTransaction` method that we created in the previous section. Just as a heads up: this section is going to be a lot of fun, as here you will really start to understand how powerful a blockchain can be and how blocks and transactions work with each other. You'll also get to learn how the transactions are recorded in the blockchain. So let's get started:

1. We're going to test our `createNewTransaction` method in our `test.js` file. In this file, we've already required our `blockchain.js` file and have made a new instance of our `Blockchain` called `bitcoin`, which we are logging out at the end of our file. Take a look at the following screenshot for a quick review:

```
1  const Blockchain = require('./blockchain');
2
3  const bitcoin = new Blockchain();
4
5              I
6
7
8
9
10
11  console.log(bitcoin);
```

2. Now, the first thing that we're going to do in our `test.js` file is create a new block using our `createNewBlock` method, similarly to what we did in the *Testing the createNewBlock method* section. Type in the following into your `test.js` file:

```
bitcoin.createNewBlock(789457, 'OIUOEDJETH8754DHKD', '78SHNEG45DER56'
);
```

3. Next, what we want to do is create some new transactions to test our `createNewTransaction` method. This `createNewTransaction` method takes in three parameters, such as `amount`, a `sender`, and the `recipient`. Let's add this transaction data to our test case:

```
bitcoin.createNewTransaction(100, 'ALEXHT845SJ5TKCJ2', 'JENN5BG5DF6HT
8NG9');
```

In the preceding line of code, we've set the amount of the transaction to 100 and the sender and recipient's address to some random hash numbers.

 You might have noticed the names ALEX and JEN in the addresses. We've added those just to simplify the identification of who the sender and recipient is. In reality, you would more than likely not have this kind of name appear at the beginning of an address. We've done this to make it easier for us to reference these addresses.

Now, let's just quickly summarize what we have done so far in our test case. Take a look at the following code block:

```
const Blockchain = require('./blockchain');

const bitcoin = new Blockchain();

bitcoin.createNewBlock(789457,'OIUOEDJETH8754DHKD','78SHNEG45DER56'
);

bitcoin.createNewTransaction(100,'ALEXHT845SJ5TKCJ2','JENN5BG5DF6HT
8NG9');


console.log(bitcoin);
```

In the preceding code, we first required the bitcoin blockchain, and then we created a new block. After that, we created a new transaction, and then we logged out the bitcoin blockchain.

When we run this test.js file, we should expect to see our bitcoin blockchain, which should have one block in the chain as well as one transaction in the pendingTransactions array because we have not mined or created a new block after creating the transaction. Let's save this file and run it to see what we get.

4. Now go to your terminal window, type in the following command, and then press *Enter*:

```
node dev/test.js
```

We get to observe the bitcoin blockchain on the terminal window, as shown in the following screenshot:

```
1. Eric@Erics-MBP-2: ~/programs/blockchain (zsh)

→ blockchain node dev/test.js
Blockchain {
  chain:
   [ { index: 1,
       timestamp: 1524002678508,
       transactions: [],
       nonce: 892348,
       hash: 'OIANS909A0S9NF',
       previousBlockHash: 'A90SDNF09AN90N' } ],
  pendingTransactions:
   [ { amount: 100,
       sender: 'ALEXSD89F9W0N90A',
       recipient: 'JENN0AN09N09A9' } ] }
```

In the output on your window and in the preceding screenshot, you can observe our chain, which has the one block that we created. In our `pendingTransactions` array, we have one pending transaction, which is the transaction we created in the test case. Looking at the output of the test, we can conclude that, so far, our `createNewTransaction` method works fine.

Adding a pending transaction to our blockchain

Now let's try to understand how we can get the `pendingTransaction` into our actual `chain` up here. The way we do that is by mining a new block or by creating a new block. Let's do that now:

1. After we create the `newTransaction`, let's create a new block using the `createNewBlock` method, as highlighted in the following code:

```
const Blockchain = require('./blockchain');

const bitcoin = new Blockchain();

bitcoin.createNewBlock(789457,'OIUOEDJETH8754DHKD','78SHNEG45DER56'
);
```

```
bitcoin.createNewTransaction(100,'ALEXHT845SJ5TKCJ2','JENN5BG5DF6HT
8NG9');
```

bitcoin.createNewBlock(548764,'AKMC875E6S1RS9','WPLS214R7T6SJ3G2');

```
console.log(bitcoin);
```

What we have done is created a block, created a transaction, and then mined a new block. Now the transaction that we created should show up in our second block because we mined a block after we created a transaction.

2. Now save the file and run the test again. Let's see what we get from this. Go to your terminal and again type in the `node dev/test.js` command and press *Enter*. You will get to observe the output that is shown in the following screenshot:

```
➜ blockchain node dev/test.js
Blockchain {
  chain:
   [ { index: 1,
       timestamp: 1524002775007,
       transactions: [],
       nonce: 892348,
       hash: 'OIANS909A0S9NF',
       previousBlockHash: 'A90SDNF09AN90N' },
     { index: 2,
       timestamp: 1524002775007,
       transactions: [Array],
       nonce: 123123,
       hash: 'JNKABSDFUBU8998H',
       previousBlockHash: '09IOANSDFN09' } ],
  pendingTransactions: [] }
```

Here, we have our entire blockchain again, which has two blocks in it because we mined two blocks. The chain has our first block (**index: 1**), which has no transactions and has our second block (**index: 2**), in which, if you look at our transactions, it says that there is an **Array** that has items in it versus a first block's transaction array, which has no items in it.

3. Now take a closer look at the second block's transaction array. We should expect to see the transaction that we had created previously. Let's make the following highlighted modification to our test case:

```
const Blockchain = require('./blockchain');

const bitcoin = new Blockchain();

bitcoin.createNewBlock(789457,'OIUOEDJETH8754DHKD','78SHNEG45DER56'
);

bitcoin.createNewTransaction(100,'ALEXHT845SJ5TKCJ2','JENN5BG5DF6HT
8NG9');

bitcoin.createNewBlock(548764,'AKMC875E6S1RS9','WPLS214R7T6SJ3G2');

console.log(bitcoin.chain[1]);
```

4. In this modification, we just log out of the second block in our chain. [1] in the code defines the position of the second block. Save this file and run it. In the output, you can observe that we are simply logging out of the second block in our chain and you can see that, for transactions, it has an array with one object in it. Check out the following screenshot:

This object is the transaction that we created in our test. What we did here was just create a transaction and then mine it by creating a new block or mining a new block, which now has our transaction in it.

Now, let's carry out a couple more examples to help clarify what is happening here. Let's take the `createNewTransaction` method and duplicate it three more times after our `createNewBlock` method. Make the modifications to the amounts as you wish to.

What's happening over here is that, from the top, we are first creating a block and then creating a transaction. We are then creating or mining a new block, so we should have one block with no transactions and another block with one transaction in it. After we create our second block, we are creating three more new transactions. At this point, all three of these new transactions should be in our `pendingTransactions` array because we are not creating a new block after we create these three transactions. Lastly, we log out of our bitcoin blockchain again. Your test should now look similar to the following:

```
const Blockchain = require('./blockchain');

const bitcoin = new Blockchain();

bitcoin.createNewBlock(789457,'OIUOEDJETH8754DHKD','78SHNEG45DER56');

bitcoin.createNewTransaction(100,'ALEXHT845SJ5TKCJ2','JENN5BG5DF6HT8NG9');

bitcoin.createNewBlock(548764,'AKMC875E6S1RS9','WPLS214R7T6SJ3G2');

bitcoin.createNewTransaction(50,'ALEXHT845SJ5TKCJ2','JENN5BG5DF6HT8NG9');
bitcoin.createNewTransaction(200,'ALEXHT845SJ5TKCJ2','JENN5BG5DF6HT8NG9');
bitcoin.createNewTransaction(300,'ALEXHT845SJ5TKCJ2','JENN5BG5DF6HT8NG9');

console.log(bitcoin);
```

Now, if we save the file and run it, we should have two blocks in our chain, and we should also have three transactions in the pendingTransactions array. Let's see what we get here. You will get to observe the following output on your screen:

```
Blockchain {
  chain:
   [ { index: 1,
       timestamp: 1524002978808,
       transactions: [],
       nonce: 892348,
       hash: 'OIANS909A0S9NF',
       previousBlockHash: 'A90SDNF09AN90N' },
     { index: 2,
       timestamp: 1524002978808,
       transactions: [Array],
       nonce: 123123,
       hash: 'JNKABSDFUBU8998H',
       previousBlockHash: '09IOANSDFN09' } ],
  pendingTransactions:
   [ { amount: 50,
       sender: 'ALEXSD89F9W0N90A',
       recipient: 'JENN0AN09N09A9' },
     { amount: 300,
       sender: 'ALEXSD89F9W0N90A',
       recipient: 'JENN0AN09N09A9' },
     { amount: 2000,
       sender: 'ALEXSD89F9W0N90A',
       recipient: 'JENN0AN09N09A9' } ] }
```

In the preceding screenshot, you can observe that we have our blockchain. In this chain, we have two blocks, just like we expected to have, and in our pendingTransactions array, we have three transactions, which are the three transactions that we had created in our test file.

What we have to do next is get these pending transactions into our chain. For that, let's mine another block. Just copy and paste the `creatNewBlock` method after the three transactions that we created and make modifications to its parameters as you wish to. When we run the test now, the three transactions that are pending should appear in our new block. Let's save the file and run the test. You will get to observe the following output:

```
→ blockchain node dev/test.js
Blockchain {
  chain:
   [ { index: 1,
       timestamp: 1524003060248,
       transactions: [],
       nonce: 892348,
       hash: 'OIANS909A0S9NF',
       previousBlockHash: 'A90SDNF09AN90N' },
     { index: 2,
       timestamp: 1524003060248,
       transactions: [Array],
       nonce: 123123,
       hash: 'JNKABSDFUBU8998H',
       previousBlockHash: '09IOANSDFN09' },
     { index: 3,
       timestamp: 1524003060248,
       transactions: [Array],
       nonce: 9878934,
       hash: '09ASF09N90ASDF',
       previousBlockHash: 'AIOS9F0AISNFAN' } ],
  pendingTransactions: [] }
```

So, we have our blockchain, which has three blocks in it. Our `pendingTransactions` array is currently empty, but where did those three transactions go? As it turns out, they should be in the last block that we created, which is the **index: 3** block. Inside of this third block we have our transactions, which should be the three transactions we just created. Let's take a deeper look at this by making a tiny modification to the last line of our test code, which is `console.log(bitcoin.chain[2]);` . The value 2 here specifies the third block in the chain. Let's save this modification and run the test again. You will get to see the third block in the chain:

```
➜ blockchain node dev/test.js
{ index: 3,
  timestamp: 1524003116642,
  transactions:
   [ { amount: 50,
       sender: 'ALEXSD89F9W0N90A',
       recipient: 'JENN0AN09N09A9' },
     { amount: 300,
       sender: 'ALEXSD89F9W0N90A',
       recipient: 'JENN0AN09N09A9' },
     { amount: 2000,
       sender: 'ALEXSD89F9W0N90A',
       recipient: 'JENN0AN09N09A9' } ],
  nonce: 9878934,
  hash: '09ASF09N90ASDF',
  previousBlockHash: 'AIOS9F0AISNFAN' }
```

In the transaction's array, you can see that we have all three of the transactions that we created. So, this is how our `createNewTransaction` and `createNewBlock` methods work with each other.

If you are having trouble understanding how both of these methods work or how they work together, we encourage you to mess around with your `test.js` file and create some new blocks, create some new transactions, log some different information out, and get a good idea of how these things work.

Hashing the data

The next method that we are going to look at and add into our blockchain data structure is called `hashBlock`. What this `hashBlock` method will do is take in a block from our blockchain and hash its data into a fixed length string. This hashed data will appear randomly.

In essence, what we're going to do is pass some blocks of data into this hash method, and in return we'll get a fixed-length string, which will simply be a hash data that is generated from the data that we passed in or from the block that we passed.

To add the `hashBlock` method to our blockchain data structure, type the following line of code after our `createNewTransaction` method:

```
Blockchain.prototype.hashBlock = function(blockdata) {

}
```

In our `hashBlock` method, `blockdata` will be the input data of our block from which we want to generate the hash.

So, how can we take a block or blocks of data and get a hashed string in return? For generating hash data, we're going to use a hashing function called **SHA256**.

Understanding the SHA256 hashing function

The **SHA256** hashing function takes in any string of text, hashes that text, and returns a fixed-length hashed string.

To get a better understanding of what hash data looks like, visit `https://passwordsgenerator.net/sha256-hash-generator/`. This is a hash generator. If you input any text into the text box, you will get hash data as the output.

For example, if we put `CodingJavaScript` into the textbox, the hash that is returned to us will look like the one highlighted in the following screenshot:

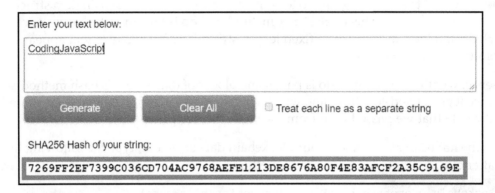

The output hash that we can observe in the preceding screenshot seems arbitrary, and thus helps in keeping the data safe. This is one of the reasons why SHA256 hashing is so secure.

Now, if we add another character to our input string or if we change our input string in any way, the entire output hash will change completely. For example, if we add an exclamation mark at the end of our input string, the output hash will entirely change. You can observe that in the following screenshot:

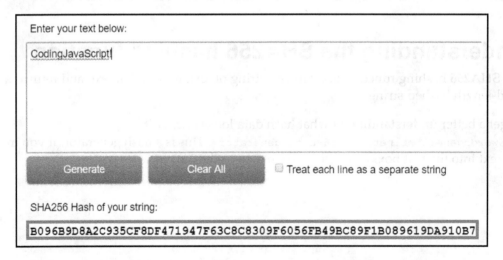

You can try experimenting by adding new characters at the end of the input string. You'll observe that as we add more or remove the characters, the entire output hash will change drastically every time, thus generating the new random patterns.

One other thing that you may want to observe related to SHA256 hashing is that with any given input, the output will always be the same. For example, for our input string, `codingJavaScript!`, you will always get the same hash output that was shown in the previous screenshot. This is another very important feature of SHA256 hashing. With any given input, the output or the hash that is returned from that input will always be the same.

So, this is how SHA256 hashing works. In the next section, we'll implement the SHA256 hashing function inside of our `hashBlock` method.

The hashBlock method

Let's build up our `hashBlock` method. Inside of this method, we want to use SHA256 hashing to hash our block data. Follow the below mentioned steps:

1. To use an SHA256 hashing function, import it as an npm library. To do that, go to Google and type SHA256 into the search bar, or visit `https://www.npmjs.com/package/sha256`. On this website, you will get to see the command that we need to type into our terminal to install SHA256. We'll have to type in the following command in our terminal:

   npm i sha 256--save

2. After doing this, press *Enter*. The `--save` in the following command will save this library as a dependency for us. Now, inside of our blockchain file structure, you may see that the `node_modules` folder has appeared. Inside of this folder is where our SHA256 library and all other dependencies have been downloaded.

3. To use this SHA256 library, we will have to import the library to our code so that we can use it. At the very start of our code, type the following line:

   ```
   const sha256 = require('sha256');
   ```

   The preceding line of code specifies that we have an SHA256 hashing function stored as the variable SHA256 in the `blockchain.js` file. By importing it, we can use that inside of our `hashBlock` method.

4. Now, the first thing that we want to do in our `hashBlock` method is to change the parameters that it takes. We're going replace the `blockData` parameter with `previousBlockHash`, `currentBlockData`, and `nonce`:

```
Blockchain.prototype.hashBlock = function(previousBlockHash,
currentBlockData, nonce) {

}
```

These three parameters will be the data that we are going to be hashing inside of our `hashBlock` method. All of this data will come from a single block in our chain and we're going to hash this data, which is essentially hashing a block. We are then going to get a hashed string in return.

5. The first thing that we want to do is change all of these pieces of data into a single string, so add the following line of code to our `hashBlock` method:

```
const dataAsString = previousBlockHash + nonce.tostring()+
JSON.stringify( currentBlockData);
```

In the preceding code, `previousBlockHash` is already a string. Our nonce is a number, so we're going to change that to a string with `toString`. Furthermore, our `currentBlockData` is going to be an object, an array of our transactions, or some kind of JSON data. It will either be an array or an object, and `JSON.stringify` will simply turn that data (as well as any object or array) into a string. Once this whole line is run, we will simply have all of the data that we passed to be concatenated into a single string.

6. Now, the next thing that we want to do is create our hash, as follows:

```
const hash = sha256(dataAsString);
```

This is how we create a hash from our block or all of the block data that we have passed into our function.

7. The last thing that we want to do is simply return the hash, so before we complete this method, add the following:

```
return hash;
```

This is how our `hashBlock` method will work. In the following section, we will test this method to see if it works perfectly.

Testing the hashBlock method

Let's test our `hashBlock` method in the `test.js` file. Similar to what we did in the previous sections, in our `test.js` file, we should be importing our blockchain data structure, creating a new instance of our blockchain, and naming it `bitcoin`. Now, let's test our `hashBlock` method:

1. For that, type in the following highlighted line of code into our `test.js` file:

```
const Blockchain = require ('./blockchain');
const bitcoin = new Blockchain ();

bitcoin.hashBlock();
```

2. Our `hashBlock` method requires three parameters: a `previousBlockHash`, `currentBlockData`, and the `nonce`. Let's define these variables above the part where we're calling our `hashBlock` method. We'll begin by defining the `previousBlockHash`:

```
const previousBlockHash = '87765DA6CCF0668238C1D27C35692E11';
```

For now, this random string/hash data will act as input for our `previousBlockHash`.

3. Next, we create the `currentBlockData` variable. This `currentBlockData` will simply be an array of all of the transactions that will be present in this block. We're simply going to use the transactions in this block as our `currentBlockData`, so in this array, we will have to make a couple of transaction objects, as follows:

```
const currentBlockData = [
    {
        amount: 10,
        sender: 'B4CEE9C0E5CD571',
        recipient: '3A3F6E462D48E9',
    }
]
```

4. Next, duplicate this transaction object at least three times to make a couple more transaction objects in the array and then make modifications to the data as you wish, aiming to change the amount and the sender's and recipient's addresses. This will make our `currentBlockData` an array that holds three transactions.

5. Finally, we have to assign the `nonce` value in our `hashBlock` method:

```
const nonce = 100;
```

6. After defining these variables, we call the `hashBlock` method and pass the `previousBlockHash` and `currentBlockData` parameters, as well as the `nonce`:

```
bitcoin.hashBlock(previousBlockHash, currentBlockData, nonce );
```

7. Furthermore, let's try to push the results onto the terminal window so that we can observe it. To do this, we'll have to make a tiny modification to our preceding code:

```
console.log(bitcoin.hashBlock(previousBlockHash, currentBlockData,
nonce));
```

In this test case, we are calling our `hashBlock` method with all of the correct parameters. When we run this file, we should get to observe the hash on the terminal window.

8. Now save this `test.js` file and run it to check whether or not we get the output that we expect it to be.

9. Go to your terminal window and type in the `node dev/test.js` command, and let's observe what results we get. You will get to observe the similar resulting hash as output of our `hashBlock` method as follows:

```
➜  blockchain git:(master) ✗ node dev/test.js
1dd6716a260b7d2382ab7ae5430103acf045ae92872266bbf1d8104b165e36bf
```

It looks like our `hashBlock` method is working pretty well.

10. Try to explore this `hashBlock` method a little more. As explained in the previous section, if we change some of the data that we are passing into the `hashBlock` method, it will result in completely changing the hash that we returned as output.

11. Now try to test this feature of hashing data by changing a letter in any of the sender's or recipient's address. Then save the file and run it by using `node dev/test.js` again. You will get to observe a totally different hash data as output, as follows:

```
→ blockchain git:(master) ✗ node dev/test.js
1dd6716a260b7d2382ab7ae5430103acf045ae92872266bbf1d8104b165e36bf
→ blockchain git:(master) ✗ node dev/test.js
a26098d56ccc4f337720e2d97f6072634df743f6db5f61a89ccac39c9d972d02
```

In the preceding screenshot, you can observe both the hash data and the differences between them.

Now, if we revert the change that we made to the sender's or recipient's address and run our hash method again, we'll get to observe the same hash that we originally got. This is because we're passing in the same data that we did the first time around. You can try experimenting with the data and try observing the output to explore the `hashBlock` method further.

After this test, we can thus conclude that our `hashBlock` method works perfectly.

What is a Proof of Work?

The next method that we are going to add to our blockchain data structure is the `proofOfWork` method. This method is very important and essential to the blockchain technology. It is because of this method that Bitcoin and many other blockchains are so secure.

Now, you must be getting curious about what a **Proof of Work** (**PoW**) actually is. Well, if we take a look at our blockchain, every blockchain is pretty much a list of blocks. Every single block has to be created and added to the chain. However, we don't just want any block to be created and added to the chain. We want to make sure that every block that is added to the chain is legitimate, has the correct transactions, and has the correct data inside of it. This is because if it doesn't have the correct transactions or the correct data, then people could fake how much Bitcoin they have and essentially cause fraud and steal money from other people. So, every time a new block is created, we first have to make sure that it is a legitimate block by mining it through PoW.

A `proofOfWork` method will take in the `currentBlockData` and the `previousBlockHash`. From this data that we supply, the `proofOfWork` method will try to generate a specific hash. This specific hash in our example is going to be a hash that starts with four zeros. So, with the given `currentBlockData` and the `previousBlockHash`, the method will somehow generate a resulting hash that begins with four zeros.

Now let's try to understand how we can do this. As we learned in the previous sections, the hash that is generated from SHA256 is pretty much random. So, if the resulting hash is pretty much random, then how can we generate a hash from our current block that starts with four zeros? The only way this can be done is by trial and error, or by guessing and checking. So, what we will have to do is run our `hashBlock` method many times until we end up getting lucky one time by generating a hash that has four zeros at the beginning.

Now, you might be wondering that the input to our `hashBlock` method are the `previousBlockHash`, `currentBlockData`, and `nonce` parameters. How will these three parameters that have been passed in once and possibly generate multiple different hashes, when, in actual fact, we're always passing exactly the same data? Furthermore, as we know from the previous section that whenever we pass in a specific piece of data, we are always going to get the same resulting hash generated from that data.

So, how can we alter this data in a way that does not change our `currentBlockData` or the `previousBlockHash`, but we still get a resulting hash that has four zeros at the beginning of it? The answer to this question is that we are going to constantly change the nonce value.

This might all seem a bit confusing right now, so let's try to clarify it by knowing what actually happens in a `proofOfWork` by breaking it down a little bit.

Essentially, what is happening in our `proofOfWork` is that we're going to repeatedly hash our block until we find the correct hash, which will be any hash that starts with four zeros. We'll be changing the input to our `hashBlock` method by constantly incrementing the nonce value. The first time that we run our `hashBlock` method, we are going to start with a nonce value of 0. Then, if that resulting hash does not have four zeros at the beginning of it, we are going to run our `hashBlock` method again, except this time we are going to increment our nonce value by 1. If we do not get the correct hash value again, we're going to increment the nonce value and try it again. If that doesn't work, we'll again increment the nonce value and try again. Then we'll continually run this `hashBlock` method until we find a hash that begins with four zeros. That is how our `proofOfWork` method will function.

You might be wondering how this `proofOfWork` method actually secures the blockchain. The reason for this is because in order to generate the correct hash, we're going to have to run our `hashBlock` method many times, and this is going to use up a lot of energy and computing power.

So, if somebody wanted to go back into the blockchain and try to change a block or the data in that block – perhaps to give themselves more Bitcoin – they would have to do a ton of calculations and use a lot of energy to create the correct hash. In most cases, going back and trying to recreate an already existing block or trying to re-mine an already existing block with your own fake data is not feasible. On top of that, not only does our `hashBlock` method take in the `currentBlockData`, it also takes in the previous `BlockHash`. This means that all of the blocks in the blockchain are linked together by their data.

If somebody tries to go back and re-mine or recreate a block that already exists, they would also have to re-mine and recreate every single block that comes after the first one that they recreated. This would take an incredible amount of calculation and energy, and is just not feasible for a well-developed blockchain. A person would have to go in, recreate a block by using a proof of work, and then recreate every block after that by doing a new proof of work for each block. This is just not feasible for any well-produced blockchain, and this is the reason why blockchain technology is so secure.

To summarize this section, what our `proofOfWork` method will basically do is repeatedly hash our `previousBlockHash`, our `currentBlockData`, and a nonce until we get an acceptable generated hash that starts with four zeros.

This might all seem overwhelming and a little bit confusing right now, but don't worry – we are going to build the `proofOfWork` method in the following section, and then we're going to test it with many different types of data. This will help you to become much more familiar with how the `proofOfWork` method functions and how it is securing the blockchain.

Creating the proofOfWork method

Let's build out the `proofOfWork` method, which we discussed in the preceding section:

1. After the `hashBlock` method, define the `proofOfWork` method as follows:

```
Blockchain.prototype.proofOfWork = function() {

}
```

2. This method takes in two parameters: `previousBlockHash` and `currentBlockData`:

```
Blockchain.prototype.proofOfWork = function( previousBlockHash,
currentBlockData) {

}
```

3. The first thing that we want to do inside of our method is define a nonce:

```
Blockchain.prototype.proofOfWork = function( previousBlockHash,
currentBlockData) {
    let nonce = 0;

}
```

4. Next, we want to hash all of our data for the first time, so type in the following highlighted line of code:

```
Blockchain.prototype.proofOfWork = function( previousBlockHash,
currentBlockData) {
    let nonce = 0;
    let hash = this.hashBlock(previousBlockHash, currentBlockData,
    nonce);
}
```

In the preceding code, you may notice that we used the term `let` because both our nonce and hash will be changing as we move through the method.

5. The next step that we want to do is constantly run the `hashBlock` method over and over again until we get a hash that starts with four zeros. We're going to do this repeated operation with the help of a `while` loop:

```
Blockchain.prototype.proofOfWork = function( previousBlockHash,
currentBlockData) {
    let nonce = 0;
    let hash = this.hashBlock(previousBlockHash, currentBlockData,
    nonce);
    while (hash.substring(0, 4) !== '0000' {
    }
}
```

6. If the hash that we created does not start with four zeros, we'll want to run our hash again, except this time with the different value of nonce. Consequently, inside of the `while` loop, add the following highlighted lines of code:

```
Blockchain.prototype.proofOfWork = function( previousBlockHash,
currentBlockData) {
    let nonce = 0;
    let hash = this.hashBlock(previousBlockHash, currentBlockData,
    nonce);
    while (hash.substring(0, 4) !== '0000' {
        nonce++;
        hash = this.hashBlock(previousBlockHash, currentBlockData,
        nonce);
    }
}
```

Inside of the `while` loop, we are running our `hashBlock` method again with all the same data, except this time our nonce is incremented and equal to 1 instead of 0. This will be the first iteration of our while loop. Now, after the first iteration, the new hash that is generated doesn't have the first four characters equal to 0000. In this case, we'll want to generate a new hash. So, our while loop will run again, the nonce value will be incremented to 2 and a new hash will be created. If that hash also does not start with four zeros then the `while` loop will run again, the nonce value will be incremented again, and the hash will be generated again.

Our loop will continue doing this until it winds up with a hash that starts with four zeros. This might take many iterations. This could happen 10 times, 10,000 times, or 100,000 times.

This loop is where all of the calculations will take place, and this is the reason why the `proofOfWork` method uses so much energy – there are a lot of calculations being made. We'll continue going through the `while` loop until we generate a suitable hash that starts with four zeros. When we finally have the correct hash, our `while` loop will stop running, and at the end of our proofOfWork, it will simply return the nonce value that gave us the valid hash:

```
Blockchain.prototype.proofOfWork = function( previousBlockHash,
currentBlockData) {
    let nonce = 0;
    let hash = this.hashBlock(previousBlockHash, currentBlockData, nonce);
    while (hash.substring(0, 4) !== '0000' {
        nonce++;
        hash = this.hashBlock(previousBlockHash, currentBlockData, nonce);
    }
    return nonce;
}
```

So, this is how our `proofOfWork` method will work and validate the hash.

In the following section, we'll test our `proofOfWork` method to make sure that it works properly. We'll also study why we return a nonce value instead of returning the hash.

Testing the proofOfWork method

Let's test our `proofOfWork` method to make sure that it works properly. We'll be testing the method in our `test.js` file. So, let's get started:

1. Open up the `test.js` file. You might observe the data in a similar way to the following screenshot, which is present in the file from the previous section, *Testing the hashBlock method*:

```js
const Blockchain = require('./blockchain');
const bitcoin = new Blockchain();

const previousBlockHash = 'OINAISDFN09N09ASDNF90N90ASNDF';
const currentBlockData = [
    {
        amount: 101,
        sender: 'N90ANS90N90ANSDFN',
        recipient: '90NA90SNDF90ANSDF09N'
    },
    {
        amount: 30,
        sender: '09ANS09DFNA8SDNF',
        recipient: 'UIANSIUDFUIABSDUIFB'
    },
    {
        amount: 200,
        sender: '89ANS89DFN98ASNDF89',
        recipient: 'AUSDF89ANSD9FNASD'
    }
];
const nonce = 100;
```

2. If you don't have any data in the `test.js` file, add this to your `test.js` file, as shown in the preceding screenshot, and then you can begin testing the data.

3. To test our `proofOfWork` method, we need the `previousBlockHash` and `currentBlockData`. So, in our test case, get rid of the nonce value and add the following lines of code to our file:

```js
console.log(bitcoin.proofOfWork(previousBlockHash,
currentBlockData));
```

Now, what we should get as a result from this `proofOfWork` method is a nonce value. What our `proofOfWork` method essentially does is test to see what the correct nonce value is to hash with our block data and our `previousBlockHash` to generate a resulting block hash that starts with four zeros.
Here, `proofOfWork` finds the correct nonce for us.

4. Save this file and run our test by typing the `node dev/test.js` command in our terminal window. After the test is run, you will observe that a number pops up as an output on the screen:

```
                                          1. Eric@Erics-MBP-2: ~/programs/blockchain (zsh)
➜  blockchain git:(master) ✗ node dev/test.js
27470
➜  blockchain git:(master) ✗ ▮
```

What this number signifies is that it took 27,470 iterations for our `proofOfWork` method to find a hash that starts with four zeros.

5. Now, to understand this whole process in-depth, what we can do is, inside of our `while` loop, log out of every hash that we try. We will have to make minor modifications to our `while` loop, as highlighted in the following code block:

```
while (hash.substring(0, 4) !== '0000' {
    nonce++;
    hash = this.hashBlock(previousBlockHash, currentBlockData,
    nonce);
    console.log(hash);
}
```

When we run our test file now, what's going to happen is we should actually get to see 27,000 different hashes logged out inside of our terminal. None of these hashes will start with four zeros, except for the last one. Only the last hash that gets logged out should start with four zeros because after our method, this will terminate and return the nonce value for which the valid hash was obtained.

Now let's save our `test.js` file again. You can now observe on your screen that we have a whole bunch of different hashes being logged out to the terminal:

```
1. Eric@Erics-MBP-2: ~/programs/blockchain (zsh)
21ccfc6aece8f9fe9c648edfebe3cf07b206027f9e5c15bafe577c479e78a097
10b80fef490747104d9cc4ce872e686ff8dbe993ff56026131481028a53787bb
889108ccd179a4eabb030413ceb7e07e020935aaec986d1b8c77b10fc3a0ea54
0c32b5ff1213e45925ac22fd1b6cc6581222ff683ad17806e97fa46a4ea1c468
efd3d3421a58415931279dc8cee7f294c5a4e35bd0bd466a7b5a6837e98d7610
cbb95fe4a2f5e42518331803d0d90d6178ada1442c3d98c302806f1f6304ed10
fc1cc7d698beb0c4f7e1f41773749e652f077ed02e26d9efda5362607d223b29
deb76b9f79ebe68d70c5e93edc8b0e172f5165f4a74cb84aa2304602c534ba14
df0f5c41501c990183f23db840570bcf83147ce9d985ca6b6261817fb0dcc098
c7cc9e990f7356c7807a5f9d292da3becbc6fdf21825555e50d53a04069a7773
ec4f27d0f44818c57d979c7edb36b1cd7c61e53c069d3bd2c565064b85a9e8c0
5901569dd2c533531e91db1c45b9e2427e1ca92e50a90f6a0c911de3da45dbb5
b9430e1a6e9732155c56a47b07c1fdb7cf6fae0eee102485093b234b1800b434
fbcd9d7e0f7fdbae01d9c0d67e619e1cbdfd674e7264fe5608596611753575c6
caf0f5d5ba5528327824ca867ae01416fef566f0081a9d9dbb1d62b6c4ff1d42
0652533d83548d19e542465a04425f9971bddd522d08722cfc8b54414e9fc3fa
90e61ddb9f5dae4113824cccbaa598097ef1119803323b619867d9a1b589917f
25f4ebd958340bb9a98c96eb7c444416e56c64a4d70558faa766938f8d428bc3
1bb8b9f4912ec555c3e42f3e9c7ba7aced3c5692165fa70af98d4dca05344f0b
0f167cecc848e7981a5918493b4002249a5a9e26f2c6d5f427a33bef801f9794
55e1dfb5969fc690a91fe8f471759d19b4db6147bbe3ca02fecf5f95a9e7806a
0000518b38c4fc4766848cf487d5afd123bf8d1e89f434c8378a86c8b938e641
27470
```

You can also observe that for every single hash that has been logged out, the beginning is never four zeros in a row until we obtain our final value.

Basically, what is happening over here is that we are generating the hash from our `currentBlockData`, `previousBlockHash`, and `nonce` of value 0. Then, for the next hash, we are incrementing the nonce by 1. So, it's all the same input data, but the nonce value is incremented until the valid hash is obtained. Finally, at 27,470, with the value of a nonce, the valid hash is obtained.

Now let's try using our `hashBlock` method. In our `dev/test.js` file, delete the `proofOfWork` method and add the following line of code:

```
console.log(bitcoin.hashBlock(previousBlockHash, currentBlockData, nonce));
```

In the preceding code, for the nonce let's input the value 27,470. This value we obtained from our `proofOfWork` method.

What we would observe as output is running the single hash with the correct nonce value that we obtained by running the `proofOfWork` method. By doing this, we should generate a hash that starts with four zeros on the first try. Let's save it and run it. Once the test is run, you will get to observe the single hash that starts with four zeros, as shown in the following screenshot:

```
→ blockchain git:(master) ✗ node dev/test.js
0000518b38c4fc4766848cf487d5afd123bf8d1e89f434c8378a86c8b938e641
```

The `proofOfWork` is a very important part of blockchain technology. It is very difficult to calculate, as you can observe from the test results – it took us more than 27,000 iterations to generate the correct hash. Consequently, a `proofOfWork` takes in a lot of energy and many calculations, and is very difficult to calculate.

Once we have the correct proof or the nonce value at which the desired hash is generated, it should be very easy for us to verify that we have the correct nonce value. We can verify this by simply passing it into our `hashBlock` method – we would obtain the hash that starts with four zeros.

It takes a lot of work to generate a proof of work, but it is very easy to verify that it is correct. So, if we ever want to go back into our blockchain and check to make sure that a block is valid, all you have to do is hash that block's data with the previous block's hash and the nonce that was generated from the `proofOfWork` when that block was mined. If this returns a valid hash to us that starts with four zeros, then we already know that the block is valid.

Thus, from our test, we can conclude that the `proofOfWork` method works as expected.

Creating a genesis block

One more thing that we would have to add to our blockchain data structure is the genesis block. But what is a genesis block? Well, a genesis block is simply the first block in any blockchain.

To create our genesis block, we are going to use the `createNewBlock` method inside of the `Blockchain()` constructor function. Go to the `dev/blockchain.js` file, and inside of the blockchain constructor function type in the following highlighted lines of code:

```
function Blockchain () {
    this.chain = [];
    this.pendingTransactions =[];
    this.createNewBlock();
}
```

As we observed in the previous section, the `createNewBlock` method takes in the value of a nonce, a `previousBlockHash`, and a hash as parameters. Since we're using the `createNewBlock` method over here to create the genesis block, we are not going to have any of those mentioned parameters. Instead, we're simply going to pass in some arbitrary parameters, as highlighted in the following code block:

```
function Blockchain () {
    this.chain = [];
    this.pendingTransactions =[];
    this.createNewBlock(100, '0', '0');
}
```

In the preceding code, we passed the nonce value as `100`, `previousBlockHash` as 0, and the hash value as 0. These are all just arbitrary values; you can add whatever value you wish to add.

Just be aware that it is okay to pass in such arbitrary parameters while creating our genesis block, but when we use the `createNewBlock` method to create new blocks, we'll have to pass the legitimate values for the parameters.

Now save the file, and let's test the genesis block in the `test.js` file.

Testing the genesis block

In the `dev/test.js` file, we will begin by importing our blockchain data structure or Blockchain constructor function, and then making a new instance of our blockchain as `bitcoin`. We're then going to log out of the bitcoin blockchain as follows:

```
const Blockchain = require ('./blockchain');
const bitcoin = new Blockchain ();

console.log(bitcoin);
```

Save this file and run the test by typing `node dev/test.js` into the terminal.

After running the test, we can observe the genesis block, as shown in the following screenshot:

```
→ blockchain git:(master) ✗ node dev/test.js
Blockchain {
  chain:
   [ { index: 1,
       timestamp: 1524168421845,
       transactions: [],
       nonce: 100,
       hash: '0',
       previousBlockHash: '0' } ],
  pendingTransactions: [] }
```

In the preceding screenshot, for the chain array, you can see that we have one block inside of the chain. This block is our genesis block and it has a nonce of 100, a hash of 0, and a `previousBlockHash` of 0. Henceforth, all of our blockchains will have a genesis block.

Summary

In this chapter, we began by building the constructor function and then moved on to create some amazing methods such as `createNewBlock`, `creatNewTransaction`, `getLastBlock`, and so on. We then learned about the hashing method, SHA256 hashing, and created a method to generate a hash for our block data. We also learned what a proof of work is and how this works. In this chapter, you also got to learn how to test the various methods that we created and check whether they are working as expected. The methods that we have learned about in this chapter will be very useful for us in further chapters when we interact more with the blockchain.

If you want to get more familiar with the blockchain data structure, it is recommended that you open up the `test.js` file, test all of the methods, try to play around with those, observe how they work together, and have fun with it.

In the next chapter, we'll be building an API to interact with and use our blockchain. That's where the real fun begins.

3
Accessing the Blockchain through an API

Building a BlockchainIn the previous chapter, we built the beginnings of our blockchain data structure. In this chapter, we're going to be building an API that will allow us to interact with our blockchain. To build the API, we will be creating a server using the Express.js library, and then we will be building three different endpoints that will allow us to interact with our blockchain.

Let's get started and build our API from scratch. In this chapter, we are going to cover the following topics:

- Setting up Express.js
- Building the API foundation
- Installing Postman and body-parser
- Building the `/blockchain` endpoint
- Building the `/transaction` endpoint
- Building the `/mine` endpoint
- Testing the endpoints

Setting up Express.js

Let's start building our API or our server to interact with our blockchain data structure. We will be building our API in a new file that we will put into our dev folder. Let's create a new file and call it api.js; this is where we will build our entire API:

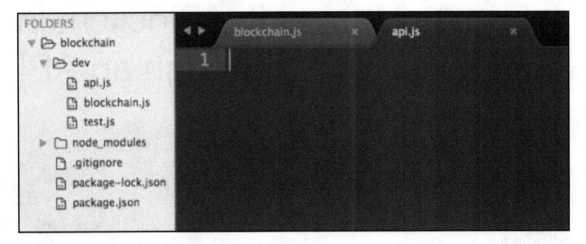

Installing Express.js

Now, we are going to use a library called Express.js to build a server or an API. Let's follow the below mentioned steps to install it:

1. So, head over to Google, search for Express.js npm, and click on the first link (https://www.npmjs.com/package/express). This should take you to the following page:

2. We have to install it as a dependency, so we must run the following command in our terminal:

```
→ blockchain git:(master) ✗ npm i express --save
npm WARN blockchain@1.0.0 No description
npm WARN blockchain@1.0.0 No repository field.

+ express@4.16.3
added 50 packages in 9.346s
→ blockchain git:(master) ✗ ▉
```

Now we have the Express library as a dependency in our project.

Using Express.js

Using Express is pretty straightforward: lets see how to use it:

1. Simply copy the example code that is present in the documentation and paste it into our `api.js` file:

```
var express = require('express')
var app = express()

app.get('/', function (req, res) {
 res.send('Hello World')
})

app.listen(3000)
```

As you can see, at the top of our file, we are requiring `express`, the library that we just downloaded, and then we are creating an `app`. This `app` will help us handle different endpoints or different routes.

For example, we have a `get` endpoint, which is just `/`. With this endpoint, we are sending back the response of `Hello World`. This whole server is listening on port 3000.

2. To start this server, we go over to our terminal and run the following command:

   node dev/api.js

3. Now our server should be running. We can test this by hitting the `get` endpoint route in our browser, and this route will simply be a localhost on port 3000.

4. Open a new tab in your browser and enter `localhost:3000`. Here you will see the text **Hello World:**

5. This is the response that was sent to us from the endpoint. We can change the text to whatever we want, so let's change `Hello World` to `Hello Coding JavaScript!`:

```
var express = require('express')
var app = express()

app.get('/', function (req, res) {
 res.send('Hello Coding JavaScript!')
})

app.listen(3000)
```

6. Now save that and restart the server by running the following command again in the terminal:

   node dev/api.js

7. Refresh the browser tab and you will see the following output:

There you go! Using Express is pretty straightforward and pretty easy. We're going to build all of our endpoints using the Express.js library.

Building the API foundation

We are going to continue building our blockchain API in this section, and then we're going to build the following three endpoints in our API to start with:

- The first endpoint is `/blockchain`, which allows us to fetch our entire blockchain so that we can look at the data that's inside of it.
- The second endpoint is `/transaction`, which allows us to create a new transaction.
- The third endpoint is `/mine`, which will allow us to mine a new block by using the `proofOfWork` method that we made in the last chapter. This is going to be a pretty powerful endpoint, and it will be fun to build.

This is basically going to be the foundation of our blockchain API. In the
`dev/networkNode.js` file, let's define these endpoints as follows:

```
const express = require('express');
const app = express();

app.get('/blockchain', function (req, res) {

});

app.post('/transaction', function(req, res) {

});

app.get('/mine', function(req, res) {

});

app,listen(3000);
```

Now, one more thing that we want to do is make some modifications to the `listen`
method:

```
app,listen(3000, function(){
    console.log('listening on port 3000...');

});
```

We have added another parameter to this method, which is a function. Inside of this
function, we are simply going to print out the `Listening on port 3000` string. The
reason that we do this is just so that when our port is actually running, we will see this text.
Let's go to our terminal and run our `api.js` file again:

```
➜  blockchain git:(master) ✗ node dev/api.js
Listening on port 3000...
```

As you can see, the preceding screenshot shows us that we are listening to port
3000. Whenever we see this text, we know that our servers are running.

Installing Postman and body-parser

In this section, we're going to work on our environment to make our development process
a little bit easier. The first thing that we're going to do is install a new package called
`nodemon`. In our `blockchain` directory in our terminal, we will write the `npm i nodemon`
`--save` command:

```
➜ blockchain git:(master) ✗ npm i nodemon --save

> fsevents@1.2.0 install /Users/Eric/programs/blockchain/node_modules/fsevents
> node install

[fsevents] Success: "/Users/Eric/programs/blockchain/node_modules/fsevents/lib/b
inding/Release/node-v57-darwin-x64/fse.node" already installed
Pass --update-binary to reinstall or --build-from-source to recompile

> nodemon@1.17.3 postinstall /Users/Eric/programs/blockchain/node_modules/nodemo
n
> node -e "console.log('\u001b[32mLove nodemon? You can now support the project
via the open collective:\u001b[22m\u001b[39m\n > \u001b[96m\u001b[1mhttps://open
collective.com/nodemon/donate\u001b[0m\n')" || exit 0

Love nodemon? You can now support the project via the open collective:
 > https://opencollective.com/nodemon/donate

npm WARN blockchain@1.0.0 No description
npm WARN blockchain@1.0.0 No repository field.

+ nodemon@1.17.3
added 13 packages, removed 1 package and updated 4 packages in 15.988s
```

Whenever we make a change in one of our files and save it, this nodemon library will automatically restart our server for us so that we don't have to go back and forth from the terminal to our code to restart the server every time we make a change.

To use nodemon, we are going to open up our `package.json` file. Where it says `"scripts"`, we're going to add a new script:

```
{
  "name": "javaScript-blockchain",
  "version": "1.0.0",
  "description": "",
  "main": "index.js",
  "scripts": {
      "test": "echo \"Error: no test specified\" && exit 1",
      "start": "nodemon --watch dev -e js dev/api.js"
  }
  "author": "",
  "license": "ISC",
  "dependencies": {
      "express": "^4.16.3",
      "nodemon": "^1.17.3",
      "sha256": "^0.2.0"
  }
}
```

We have added `"start": "nodemon --watch dev -e js dev/api.js"`. This means that when we run the `start` command, we want `nodemon` to watch our `dev` folder and keep an eye on all of our JavaScript files. Whenever one of these JS files is changed and saved, we want nodemon to restart our `dev/api.js` file for us. Save the `package.json` file. Now, whenever we make a change inside of our `dev` folder and save it, our server will restart itself. Let's test this out.

Let's go to our terminal. Our server should now be using nodemon:

```
→ blockchain git:(master) ✗ npm start

> blockchain@1.0.0 start /Users/Eric/programs/blockchain
> nodemon --watch dev -e js dev/api.js

[nodemon] 1.17.3
[nodemon] to restart at any time, enter `rs`
[nodemon] watching: /Users/Eric/programs/blockchain/dev/**/*
[nodemon] starting `node dev/api.js`
Listening on port 3000...
```

We have started the server by using the `npm start` command. You can see that this is
listening on port `3000`. Whenever we make a change in one of our JS files and save it, we
will see that our server restarts itself:

```
[nodemon] starting `node dev/api.js`
Listening on port 3000...
[nodemon] restarting due to changes...
[nodemon] starting `node dev/api.js`
Listening on port 3000...
```

As you can see, the server is listening to port `3000` again. This is just a tool that we use to
make development slightly easier for us. Now, one other tool that we want to use is called
Postman.

Installing Postman

The Postman tool allows us to make calls to any of our post endpoints, as well as send data
into these endpoints with our requests. Let's understand how to install it:

1. Head over to `https://www.getpostman.com` and download the app. Once you
   have downloaded the app, we can run through a little test trial of how we can
   use this Postman app to hit our `/transaction` endpoint.

2. Open the Postman app after downloading it. You will see something similar to the following screenshot:

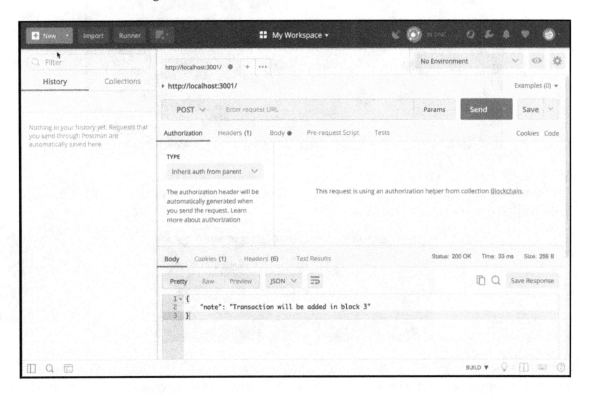

3. Now, in the Postman app we're going to make a post request to `http://localhost:3000/transaction`:

4. To test that the `/transaction` endpoint is working, let's send something back in the output. In our `/transaction` endpoint, we have added the following line:

```
app.post('/transaction', function(req, res) {
    res.send('It works!!!');
});
```

5. Let's save the file, and now when we hit this endpoint, we should get the text `It works!!!` returned to us. Click on the **Send** button, and you will get the output, as shown in the following screenshot:

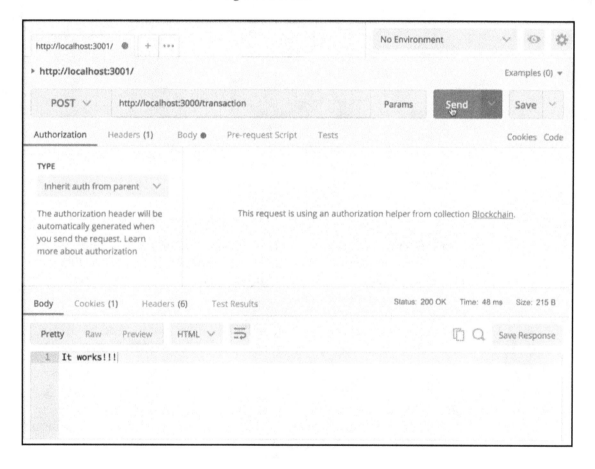

6. Now, most of the time we hit a `post` endpoint in our API, we are going to want to send data to it. For example, when we hit the `/transaction` endpoint, we want to create a new transaction. Consequently, we have to send the transaction data, such as the amount for the transaction, the sender, and the recipient to the `/transaction` endpoint. We can do this by using Postman, and it's actually pretty straightforward. What we're going to do here is send some information in the body of our post request. You can do that by clicking on the **Body** tab:

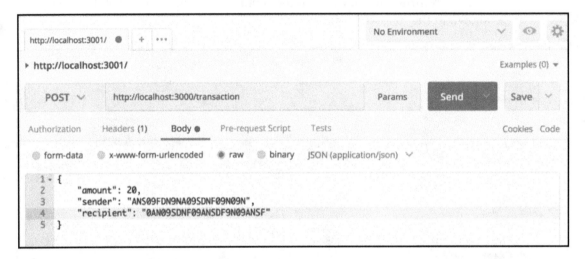

7. Next, make sure that the **raw** option is checked and **JSON (application/json)** is selected from the dropdown list. You can also see that we have made a JSON object and put some data in it. We have added the `amount` as `20` bitcoins, the address of `sender`, and the address of `recipient`.

> **TIP**
>
> Remember that everything has to be in JSON format, so we need all of our quotations to be in double quotes or the terms won't work.

8. To test whether or not we are receiving all of this information inside of our endpoint, we are going to print out the entire `req.body`. The `req.body` is simply the information that we created in the JSON object:

```
app.post('/transaction', function(req, res) {
    console.log(req.body);
    res.send(`The amount of the transaction is ${req.body.amount}
    bitcoin.`);
});
```

As you can see, we have also sent some different information back in the response. We have added a sentence in back ticks, and we also did some string interpolation with ${req.body.amount}, which will return just the amount.

9. Now, for ${req.body.amount} to work, we need to install another library in order to access this information. Let's go back in our terminal; we're going to quit the current process where we were listening to port 3000 and we're going to install a package called body-parser:

```
➜ blockchain git:(master) ✗ npm i body-parser --save
npm WARN blockchain@1.0.0 No description
npm WARN blockchain@1.0.0 No repository field.

+ body-parser@1.18.2
updated 1 package in 4.57s
```

10. Now let's start our server up again with npm start.

11. When it comes to using body-parser, we simply want to import this at the top of our file after the line where we imported app:

```
const express = require('express');
const app = express();
const bodyParser = require('body-parser');

app.use(bodyParser.json());
app.use(bodyParser.urlencoded({ extended: false }));
```

To use this body-parser library, we have added the next two lines. All these two lines is doing are stating that if a request comes in with JSON data or with form data, we simply want to parse that data so that we can access it in any of the endpoints. So, with any endpoint we hit, our data is first going to go through the body-parser so that we can access the data and is then used in whichever endpoint will be receiving it.

12. Now that we're using `body-parser`, we should be able to access the amount. Let's save the `api.js` file and try to send the request, as follows:

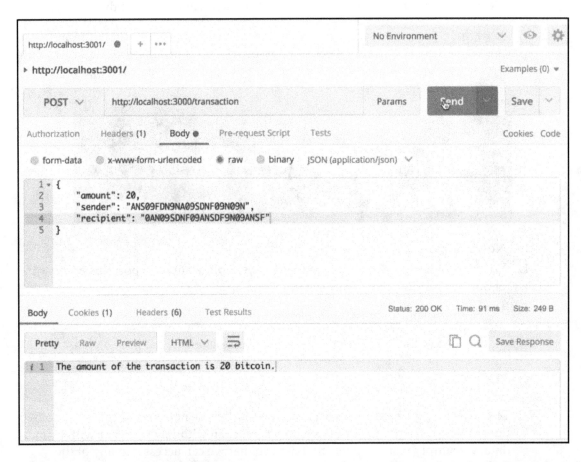

It worked! We got the string returned, which states that **The amount of the transaction is 20 bitcoin.**

In our terminal, since we logged out of the entire `req.body`, we can see that the entire information regarding the amount, sender, and recipient is displayed:

```
[nodemon] 1.17.3
[nodemon] to restart at any time, enter `rs`
[nodemon] watching: /Users/Eric/programs/blockchain/dev/**/*
[nodemon] starting `node dev/api.js`
Listening on port 3000...
[nodemon] restarting due to changes...
[nodemon] starting `node dev/api.js`
Listening on port 3000...
{ amount: 20,         I
  sender: 'ANS09FDN9NA09SDNF09N09N',
  recipient: '0AN09SDNF09ANSDF9N09ANSF' }
```

Great! Now, one more important thing to note is that throughout the rest of this chapter, you should always have your server running, which means you should always run the `npm start` command so that we can use our API, hit the different endpoints, and test it to see if it works.

Building the /blockchain endpoint

Let's continue building our blockchain API. In this section, we are going to interact with our `/blockchain` endpoint. This means that we will have to import our blockchain from our `blockchain.js` file:

```
const Blockchain = require('./blockchain');
```

We have now imported our blockchain data structure or our blockchain constructor function. Next, we want to make an instance of our blockchain. We can do that as follows:

```
const bitcoin = new Blockchain();
```

Now we have an instance of our blockchain constructor function and we have called it `bitcoin`. You can call this whatever you want, but I'm just going to call it `bitcoin` to keep it simple.

Let's build on our `/blockchain` endpoint. All this endpoint is going to do is send our entire blockchain back to whoever called this endpoint. To do that, we are going to add a line that will send the response:

```
app.get('/blockchain', function(req, res) {
    res.send(bitcoin);
});
```

Believe it or not, that's all we're going to do for this endpoint.

Testing the /blockchain endpoint

Now we can test whether or not this endpoint works by using it in our browser:

1. Let's go to our browser and hit `localhost:3000/blockchain`:

```
←  →  C  ⓘ localhost:3000/blockchain

{"chain":[{"index":1,"timestamp":1524252384868,"transactions":
[],"nonce":100,"hash":"0","previousBlockHash":"0"}],"pendingTransactions":[]}
```

2. As you can see, we get our entire blockchain back. Now, you might have noticed that this is a little bit difficult to read, so to make it readable, let's download a Chrome extension called **JSON formatter**. You can Google this and add the extension to your Chrome browser. Once installed, refresh the page again and you will get the following output:

```
←  →  C  ⓘ localhost:3000/blockchain

▼ {
   ▼ "chain": [
      ▼ {
            "index": 1,
            "timestamp": 1524252384868,
            "transactions": [],
            "nonce": 100,
            "hash": "0",
            "previousBlockHash": "0"
         }
      ],
      "pendingTransactions": []
   }
```

As you can see, we get our data back in a much more readable format, which is in JSON format. You can see that we have `chain`, which has one item in it – our genesis block – and we also have the `pendingTransaction` block. This is pretty cool, and we can tell that our `/blockchain` endpoint is working because we get our entire blockchain back.

Building the /transaction endpoint

In this section, we are going to build our transaction endpoint. Let's follow the below mentioned steps:

1. Before we start, please make sure that whenever you are working on our blockchain you have your server running. We can do that by running the `npm start` command in our terminal.

2. Let's head over to our `api.js` file and build our transaction endpoint. First of all, take out the example code that we added earlier in the `/transaction` endpoint and create a new transaction in our blockchain. To do that, we are going to use our `createNewTransaction` method in the `blockchain.js` file that we built in Chapter 2, *Building a Blockchain*.

3. As you know, our `createNewTransaction` method takes in three parameters: `amount`, `sender`, and `recipient`:

```
Blockchain.prototype.createNewTransaction = function(amount,
sender, recipient) {
  const newTransaction = {
    amount: amount,
    sender: sender,
    recipient: recipient
  };

  this.pendingTransactions.push(newTransaction);

  return this.getLastBlock()['index'] + 1;
};
```

4. This method returns the block number or the index that our new transaction will be added to. This is all that we need in order to create a transaction, so in our `/transaction` endpoint, we are going to add the following line:

```
app.post('/transaction', function(req, res) {
  const blockIndex = bitcoin.createNewTransaction(req.body.amount,
    req.body.sender, req.body.recipient)
});
```

5. In our endpoint, we're going to assume that all of this data is being sent in with the `req.body` from whoever is calling this endpoint. The result will be saved in `blockIndex`, and that is what we are going to send back to whoever calls this endpoint. We will be sending it back as a `note`:

```
app.post('/transaction', function(req, res) {
  const blockIndex = bitcoin.createNewTransaction(req.body.amount,
  req.body.sender, req.body.recipient)
    res.json({ note:`Transaction will be added in block
    ${blockIndex}.`});
});
```

As you can see, the note will tell us which block the transaction will be added to. We have used string interpolation to pass the `blockIndex` value. Let's save this file and test this endpoint using Postman.

Testing the /transaction endpoint

Now let's head over to Postman and apply settings similar to the ones that we set earlier:

We have selected the **POST** request, and we are targeting the /transaction endpoint. In the **Body** tab, we have checked **raw**, and the text has been selected to JSON format. We have passed in the values for amount, sender, and recipient in the JSON object, which will be our req.body, and on this object we will send all of our transaction data. With the help of req.body, which was mentioned in our /transaction endpoint, we can access the amount, the address of the sender, and the recipient.

Now let's test this endpoint:

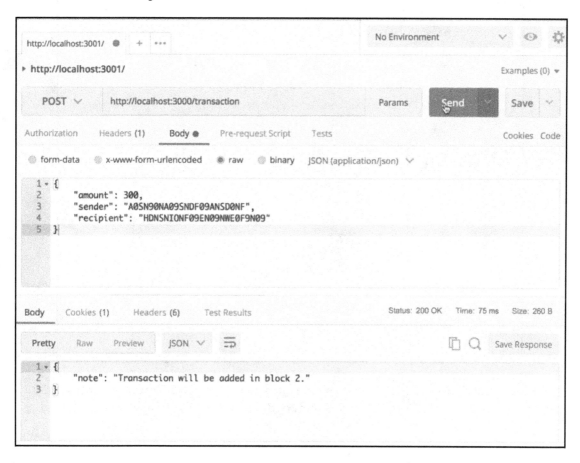

As you can see, when we clicked on the **Send** button on Postman, we got the output as **Transaction will be added in block 2**. The reason we got block 2 here is that one block had already been created when we initiated our blockchain, which created the genesis block. Consequently, this transaction got added to block 2.

One other way that we can test to make sure that this endpoint worked correctly is by hitting our /blockchain endpoint. When we hit this endpoint, we should expect to get our entire blockchain returned to us. In that blockchain, there should be a single block – our genesis block – and there should be one pending transaction, which is the transaction that we just created. Let's head over to the browser and go to localhost:3000/blockchain:

```
←  →  C  ⓘ localhost:3000/blockchain

▼ {
  ▼ "chain": [
    ▼ {
          "index": 1,
          "timestamp": 1524333137461,
          "transactions": [],
          "nonce": 100,
          "hash": "0",
          "previousBlockHash": "0"
      }
    ],
  ▼ "pendingTransactions": [
    ▼ {
          "amount": 300,
          "sender": "A0SN90NA09SNDF09ANSD0NF",
          "recipient": "HDNSNIONF09EN09NWE0F9N09"
      }
    ]
  }
```

As you can see, the entire object is our whole blockchain – the first part is our chain that has the genesis block, and the second part is our pending transaction, which we just created. Our /transaction endpoint works perfectly.

Building the /mine endpoint

Let's build the final endpoint for our blockchain API: the mine endpoint, this will mine and create a new block:

1. To create a new block, we are going to use our `createNewBlock` method, which we already defined in our `blockchain.js` file. Let's go to our `api.js` file and create a new block inside the `/mine` endpoint:

```
app.get('/mine', function(req, res) {
    const newBlock = bitcoin.createNewBlock();
});
```

2. This `createNewBlock` method takes in three parameters: `nonce`, `previousBlockHash`, and `hash`:

```
Blockchain.prototype.createNewBlock = function(nonce,
previousBlockHash, hash) {
  const newBlock = {
    index: this.chain.length + 1,
    timestamp: Date.now(),
    transactions: this.pendingTransactions,
    nonce: nonce,
    hash: hash,
    previousBlockHash: previousBlockHash
  };

  this.pendingTransactions = [];
  this.chain.push(newBlock);

  return newBlock;
};
```

3. Now we have to do calculations to get all these three pieces of data, so let's do that. Let's start by getting the previous block so that we can get its hash:

```
app.get('/mine', function(req, res) {
  const lastBlock = bitcoin.getLastBlock();
  const previousBlockHash = lastBlock['hash'];
```

As you can see, we have created `lastBlock`, which is the last block in our chain – or the previous block to our new block. To get the last block's `hash`, we have created `previousBlockHash`. With that, we can now have our `previousBlockHash`, which is one of the parameters that we need for our `createNewBlock` method next.

4. Next, let's get our `nonce`. To produce a `nonce` for our block, we need to generate a `proofOfWork`, which we created in the `blockchain.js` file:

```
Blockchain.prototype.proofOfWork = function(previousBlockHash,
currentBlockData) {
  let nonce = 0;
  let hash = this.hashBlock(previousBlockHash, currentBlockData,
  nonce);
  while (hash.substring(0, 4) !== '0000') {
    nonce++;
    hash = this.hashBlock(previousBlockHash, currentBlockData,
    nonce);
  }

  return nonce;
};
```

5. In our `/mine` endpoint, we will add the following line:

```
const nonce = bitcoin.proofOfWork(previousBlockHash,
currentBlockData);
```

6. So, from our `proofOfWork` method we will get a `nonce` returned to us. let's save that as our `nonce` variable. Our `proofOfWork` method takes in two parameters: `previousBlockHash`, which we already have, and `currentBlockData`. Let's define our `currentBlockData`:

```
const currentBlockData = {
    transactions: bitcoin.pendingTransactions,
    index: lastBlock['index'] + 1
  };
```

We have our `currentBlockData` as an object, and this consists of the data. This data will simply consist of the `transactions` in this block, and also an `index`, which is the index of the new block that we are going to create; the index of our `lastBlock` plus 1. The `currentBlockData` object is simply going to be the `transactions` that are present in this new block and its `index`. With this, we can now calculate our `nonce`, as we have with our `previousBlockHash` and `currentBlockData`.

7. Now, the final parameter that our `createNewBlock` method has to take in is a `hash` of this new block, so let's calculate that now. To create a hash of this new block, we are going to use our `hashBlock` method. We are going to add the following line in our `/mine` endpoint:

```
const blockHash = bitcoin.hashBlock(previousBlockHash,
currentBlockData, nonce);
```

As you know, we have already created the `hashBlock` method in the `blockchain.js` file. This method accepts three parameters: `previousBlockHash`, `currentBlockData`, and `nonce`. We already have all of these parameters, so we are calling it and saving the results in a variable called `blockHash`.

8. We now have all of the parameters that we need to run our `createNewBlock` method, so let's assign those:

```
const newBlock = bitcoin.createNewBlock(nonce, previousBlockHash,
blockHash);
```

What's happening here is pretty awesome. As you can see, there are a lot of different calculations that go into creating this new block, and we are able to make all of these calculations by using our blockchain data structure. This is a pretty powerful data structure, and our blockchain can now mine new blocks by using `proofOfWork`, which is similar to how many other blockchains function as well.

9. At this point, we have created our new block, and all we really have left to do is send the response back to whoever mined this block. Next, we will be adding the following line in our `/mine` endpoint:

```
res.json({
  note: "New block mined successfully",
  block: newBlock
});
```

We are simply sending back a note that says **New block mined successfully**, as well as stating the `newBlock` that we just created. Now, sending back this `newBlock` is not going to affect our blockchain in any way. We are sending back the `newBlock` so that the person who created or mined this new block knows what it looks like.

10. Now there is one thing left that we have to do: Every time someone mines a new block, they get a reward for creating that new block. All we have to do is make a transaction and send the person who mined this new block a little bit of bitcoin as their reward. To do that, inside the `/mine` endpoint, we are going to create a new transaction:

```
bitcoin.createNewTransaction(12.5, "00", nodeAddress);
```

Currently, in 2018, there is a 12.5 bitcoin reward for mining a new block in the real bitcoin blockchain. Just to stay consistent with the real bitcoin, we're going to make our reward `12.5` bitcoin too. As a sender address, we have put the value 00,. This way, whenever we are looking at transactions on our network, we know that if a transaction is made from the address 00, it is a mining reward.

Now all we need is a recipient's address, `nodeAddress`. We need to send `12.5` bitcoins to whoever mined a new block – but how can we find that? Well, we're going to be sending this reward to the current node that we are on, which is this whole API file that we are working on. We can treat this entire API as a network node in the bitcoin blockchain.

In future chapters, we're going to have multiple instances of our API, and they are going to act as different network nodes in the big clean blockchain. Right now, whenever we hit any of the endpoints we created, we are always only communicating with this one network node. However, since we know that all blockchain technology is decentralized and hosted across many different network nodes, we are going to be creating more network nodes as we proceed further. But for now, our entire blockchain is hosted solely on this one network node.

Now, any time we hit the `/mine` endpoint, we want to reward this node for mining the new block. To give this node the `12.5` bitcoin reward that it deserves, we need an address to send the bitcoin to, so let's create an address for this node now.

To create an address for this node, we are going to import a new library called `uuid` using our terminal:

```
→ blockchain git:(master) ✗ npm i uuid --save
npm WARN blockchain@1.0.0 No description
npm WARN blockchain@1.0.0 No repository field.

+ uuid@3.2.1
added 1 package in 5.117s
→ blockchain git:(master) ✗ npm start
```

Once you have typed in the `npm i uuid --save` command and hit *Enter*, the package will be added. You can start the server again with the `npm start` command.

Now let's import our new `uuid` library at the top section of our `api.js` file:

```
const uuid = require('uuid/v1');
```

As you can see, we have imported version 1 of the `uuid` library. This library creates a unique random string for us, and we're going to use that string as this network node's address. For that, we are going to add the following line:

```
const nodeAddress = uuid().split('-').join('');
```

One thing that we want to alter about the string that we get from this library is that there are a couple of dashes present – we don't want any dashes in our address. Here, we're simply going to split that string on all of the dashes and then rejoin it with an empty string that's been passed in. The `nodeAddress` that we are going to get is a random string that is guaranteed to be unique to a very high percentage. We really want this string to be unique because we don't want to have two nodes with the same address, otherwise we would end up sending bitcoin to the wrong people and that wouldn't be good. Now we can simply pass this `nodeAddress` variable into our `createNewTransaction` method.

In the next section, we will test our `/mine` endpoint, along with our `/transaction` and `/blockchain` endpoints, to make sure that they all work and interact correctly.

Testing the endpoints

In this section, we're going to be testing our `/mine` endpoint, along with our `/transaction` and `/blockchain` endpoints, to make sure that everything works well together.

 Before we test, it would be a good idea to take out the `console.log` statement in the `proofOfWork` method. This is because having it will just make your program work harder, and it will therefore take more time to calculate things.

/mine endpoint testing

First, let's test the /mine endpoint that we just built in our last section. Let's head over to our browser and hit localhost:3000/blockchain:

```
←  →  C   ⓘ localhost:3000/blockchain

▼ {
    ▼ "chain": [
        ▼ {
              "index": 1,
              "timestamp": 1524352449204,
              "transactions": [],
              "nonce": 100,
              "hash": "0",
              "previousBlockHash": "0"
          }
      ],
      "pendingTransactions": []
  }
```

Right now, we have our entire blockchain, in which the chain has one block in it – our genesis block – and we also have no pending transactions.

Now let's open another tab and hit our /mine endpoint. This should mine and create a new block for us:

```
←  C  ① localhost:3000/mine

{
    "note": "New block mined successfully",
    "block": {
        "index": 2,
        "timestamp": 1524352507191,
        "transactions": [
            {
                "amount": 12.5,
                "sender": "00",
                "recipient": "b1fa303045b911e8b0e0c1fe1fbdc17a"
            }
        ],
        "nonce": 18140,
        "hash": "0000b9135b054d1131392c9eb9d03b0111d4b516824a03c35639e12858912100",
        "previousBlockHash": "0"
    }
}
```

We got our note that says **New block mined successfully**. We also got our new block back, and we can see all of the data that's on our block. It has a hash in it, and it also has the hash of the previous block, which is the genesis block, and one transaction in it. You might be thinking, we didn't create a transaction, so where did this transaction come from? This transaction is actually the mining reward that we put into our endpoint, which has the 12.5 bitcoin mining reward transaction. It looks like our mining endpoint worked well.

Testing the / blockchain endpoint

To test and ensure that we did create this new block, we can head back over to our
/blockchain endpoint and refresh the page:

```
← C ⓘ localhost:3000/blockchain                                                    ⊕
▼ {
  ▼ "chain": [
    ▼ {
          "index": 1,
          "timestamp": 1524352449204,
          "transactions": [],
          "nonce": 100,
          "hash": "0",
          "previousBlockHash": "0"
      },
    ▼ {
          "index": 2,
          "timestamp": 1524352507191,
        ▼ "transactions": [
          ▼ {
                "amount": 12.5,
                "sender": "00",
                "recipient": "b1fa303045b911e8b0e0c1fe1fbdc17a"
            }
          ],
          "nonce": 18140,
          "hash": "0000b9135b054d1131392c9eb9d03b0111d4b516824a03c35639e12858912100",
          "previousBlockHash": "0"
      }
    ],
    "pendingTransactions": []
  }
```

It worked. We now have two blocks in our chain: one is the genesis block and the other is the one we just created. The second block also has the transaction in it, which has the reward.

Let's mine another block to test that again. Head over to our `/mine` endpoint and refresh it:

```
{
    "note": "New block mined successfully",
    "block": {
        "index": 3,
        "timestamp": 1524352636155,
        "transactions": [
            {
                "amount": 12.5,
                "sender": "00",
                "recipient": "b1fa303045b911e8b0e0c1fe1fbdc17a"
            }
        ],
        "nonce": 92894,
        "hash": "00002778916a7dadc7260a1b6cff17be291bda44445d157e48da55fe9dbb06b3",
        "previousBlockHash": "0000b9135b054d1131392c9eb9d03b0111d4b516824a03c35639e12858912100"
    }
}
```

We just mined another block, which is our third block. We can see that we get the `timestamp`, and another transaction, which is the mining reward, and also we have the rest of our data. Now let's head back to our `/blockchain` endpoint and refresh it:

```
←  C  ⓘ localhost:3000/blockchain                                    ⊕ ☆   ▦ ◆ ▣

              "nonce": 100,
              "hash": "0",
              "previousBlockHash": "0"
          },
        ▾ {
              "index": 2,
              "timestamp": 1524352507191,
            ► "transactions": [ … ], // 1 item
              "nonce": 18140,
              "hash": "0000b9135b054d1131392c9eb9d03b0111d4b516824a03c35639e12858912100",
            ▸"previousBlockHash": "0"
          },
        ▾ {

              "index": 3,
              "timestamp": 1524352636155,
            ▾ "transactions": [
              ▾ {
                    "amount": 12.5,
                    "sender": "00",
                    "recipient": "b1fa303045b911e8b0e0c1fe1fbdc17a"
                }
              ],
              "nonce": 92894,
              "hash": "00002778916a7dadc7260a1b6cff17be291bda44445d157e48da55fe9dbb06b3",
              "previousBlockHash": "0000b9135b054d1131392c9eb9d03b0111d4b516824a03c35639e12858912100"
          }
```

As you can see, we have all three blocks. Block 3 is the one that we just created, and it has our mining reward transaction in it. One more thing to notice is that our `previousBlockHash` actually aligns with our block 2's `hash`. This is helping to secure our blockchain, which is good.

Testing the /transaction endpoint

Now let's create some transactions with our /transaction endpoint. For this, head over to Postman, make sure that the settings are the same as before, and make the following changes:

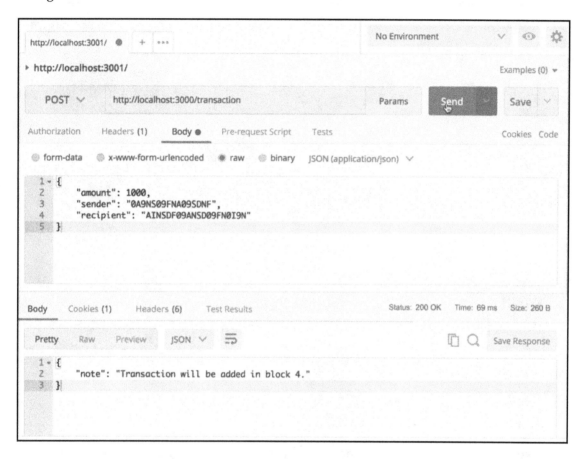

We have set the amount to 1000 bitcoins. We'll leave the sender and the recipient address as they are, but you can change it to whatever you want. Once we post to the /transaction endpoint, in return we should get the text transaction that will be added in block 4, which we did. This transaction got added to block 4 because we already have three blocks in our chain.

Let's make another example transaction. Here we will change the amount to 50 bitcoins, and we will make some changes to the address of the sender and the recipient. So when we send this request, we should get the same response: **Transaction will be added in block 4.** This occurs because we haven't mined a new block yet. Let's try this out:

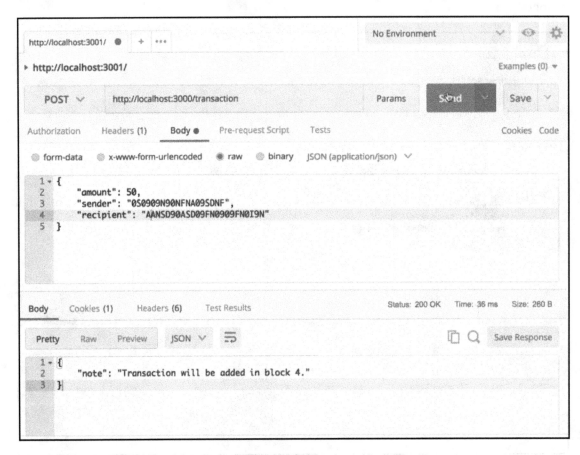

That worked. Now let's head over and get our entire blockchain again. This time, we should expect to get the same blockchain and the two pending transactions that we just created. Let's refresh the page and see the output:

```
        "pendingTransactions": [
            {
                "amount": 1000,
                "sender": "0A9NS09FNA09SDNF",
                "recipient": "AINSDF09ANSD09FN0I9N"
            },
            {
                "amount": 50,
                "sender": "0S0909N90NFNA09SDNF",
                "recipient": "AANSD90ASD09FN0909FN0I9N"
            }
        ]
    }
```

You will notice that this has three blocks and two pending transactions. Now, if we head over to our /mine endpoint and refresh the page, these two pending transactions will be added to block 4:

```
← C  ① localhost:3000/mine                                    Q ☆       Raw
{
    "note": "New block mined successfully",
    "block": {
        "index": 4,
        "timestamp": 1524352987262,
        "transactions": [
            {
                "amount": 1000,
                "sender": "0A9NS09FNA09SDNF",
                "recipient": "AINSDF09ANSD09FN0I9N"
            },
            {
                "amount": 50,
                "sender": "0S0909N90NFNA09SDNF",
                "recipient": "AANSD90ASD09FN0909FN0I9N"
            },
            {
                "amount": 12.5,
                "sender": "00",
                "recipient": "b1fa303045b911e8b0e0c1fe1fbdc17a"
            }
        ],
        "nonce": 78444,
        "hash": "00009a2d2b5b354b48dc590afcfc73213043bd1c002398ff69f65b5dc673da7c",
        "previousBlockHash": "00002778916a7dadc7260a1b6cff17be291bda44445d157e48da55fe9dbb06b3"
    }
}
```

We have successfully mined a new block. It's got our data, and it also has three transactions. The first two transactions are the ones we created in Postman, and the third one is our mining reward transaction. Now, if we go back to our `/blockchain` endpoint and refresh it, we will see that the two pending transactions are gone and that they have been added to block 4:

```
←  C  ⓘ localhost:3000/blockchain                                    ⊕ ☆    ▣ ◆ ▣
    ▼ {
        "index": 4,
        "timestamp": 1524352987262,
      ▼ "transactions": [
        ▼ {
              "amount": 1000,
              "sender": "0A9NS09FNA09SDNF",
              "recipient": "AINSDF09ANSD09FNOI9N"
          },
        ▼ {
              "amount": 50,
              "sender": "0S0909N90NFNA09SDNF",
              "recipient": "AANSD90ASD09FN0909FNOI9N"
          },
        ▼ {
              "amount": 12.5,
              "sender": "00",
              "recipient": "b1fa303045b911e8b0e0c1fe1fbdc17a"
          }
        ],
        "nonce": 78444,
        "hash": "00009a2d2b5b354b48dc590afcfc73213043bd1c002398ff69f65b5dc673da7c",
        "previousBlockHash": "00002778916a7dadc7260a1b6cff17be291bda44445d157e48da55fe9dbb06b3"
      }
    ],
    "pendingTransactions": []
  }
```

As you can see, block 4 has all three transactions, and our `pendingTransactions` is empty now. It worked out well. Now, I would encourage you to create a couple more transactions and mine another block just to make sure that everything is working properly.

By building this whole API and blockchain and really understanding how the code works, it becomes a lot easier to understand how the blockchain technology actually works, and you also realize that a lot of it isn't actually so complicated.

At any point while you are testing these endpoints, if you make changes to a file and save it, then the server will restart. This will result in a new instance of blockchain, which means that everything you have created so far will be cleared out.

Summary

In this chapter, we learned how to set up Express.js in our project, as well as how to use it to build our API/Server. Then we installed Postman and understood how to use it to test our endpoints. After this, we moved on to build various endpoints of our server and tested those to verify whether or not they were working properly.

In the next chapter, we will be creating a network of nodes or a decentralized network to host our blockchain, just like the ones that are hosted in the real world.

4
Creating a Decentralized
Blockchain Network

In this chapter, let's focus on building a decentralized blockchain network. The way that our blockchain works right now is that we have a single blockchain, and the only way to access it is through the API: our single server. This server is very centralized, which is not beneficial because the API is in total control of the blockchain and the data that gets added to it.

In the real world, all blockchain technology is hosted across a decentralized network. In this chapter, that's what we're going to focus on building. We'll build a decentralized blockchain network by creating various instances of the API. Each of these instances of the API are going to be a network node in our blockchain network. All of these nodes will work together to host our blockchain.

In this way, it's not just a single network node that has total control over our blockchain. Instead, our blockchain is hosted across the entire decentralized network. This way, if there's one bad player in our network, or somebody who is trying to cheat the system, we can refer to the other network nodes to see what the real data should be inside of our blockchain and what our blockchain should actually look like.

Having our blockchain hosted across a decentralized network is very powerful because it vastly increases the security of our blockchain, and therefore we don't have to just trust one single entity with all of our data.

In this chapter, we'll cover the following topics:

- Learning how to create and test multiple nodes
- Adding the `currentNodeUrl` to our network
- Adding new endpoints for the decentralized network
- Building the `/register-and-broadcast-node` endpoint
- Building and testing the `/register-node` endpoint

- Adding and testing the `/register-nodes-bulk` endpoint
- Testing all of the network endpoints

Let's get started with creating our decentralized network.

Creating multiple nodes

Let's begin by building the decentralized network:

1. The first thing that we'll have to do to create our decentralized blockchain network is make some modifications to our `api.js` file.

2. In our decentralized network, we're going to have multiple instances of our API, and each one of them will act as a network node. Since we'll be dealing with multiple network nodes, it will be better to rename our `api.js` file to `networkNode.js` for easy reference.

3. To set up the decentralized network, we'll have to run the `networkNode.js` file multiple times. Each time we run the file, we want it to act as a different network node. Let's do this by running the file on different ports every time we run it. To have a different ports value every time, we'll have to make port a variable. To do this, add the following line at the start of the code in our `dev/networkNode.js`:

   ```
   const port = process.argv[2];
   ```

4. Next, go to the `package.json` file and make modifications to the `start` command. What we'll do here is go to the end of our command and pass a variable for the port number on which we want a network node to run. In our example, we want to run our network node to run on port number `3001`. Consequently, pass `3001` as a variable at the end of the start command:

   ```
   "start": "nodemon --watch dev -e js dev/api.js 3001"
   ```

To get access to this variable, we passed the `process.argv` variable in our `networkNode.js` file. So, what is the `process.argv` variable? This variable simply refers to the `start` command that we run to start our server.

You can think of the preceding `start` command as an array of elements. The first and the second elements of the command are comprised of `"nodemon --watch dev -e js dev/api.js`, and the third element of the command is the `3001` variable.

TIP

If you want to add more variables to the command, you can simply make a space and then add more variables to it.

Consequently, to access the port variable in the `start` command, we passed the variable as `process.argv [2]` because this array starts with a 0 index and our port variable is the third element in the start command. To simplify this, we can access the `3001` variable by stating `process.argv` at position 2. As a result, we gain access to our `port` variable inside of our `dev/networkNode.js` file.

5. Next, we want to use the `port` variable. Therefore, in the `dev/networkNode.js` file, go to the bottom, where we have mentioned the following code:

```
app.listen(3000, function() {
    console.log('Listening on port 3000...');
});
```

6. Once you have found this, make the following highlighted modifications to it:

```
app.listen(port, function() {
    console.log(`Listening on port ${port}...`);
});
```

In the preceding block of code, we replaced the hardcoded `3000` port number with our `port` variable. We also changed `Listening on port 3000...` to `Listening on port ${port}...` by using string interpolation and passing the port variable. Now, when we run the `networkNode.js` file, it should be listening on port `3001` instead of port `3000`.

7. One tiny thing that we need to change before we run the `networkNode.js` file is that in the `package.json` file in the `start` command, we'll have to change the name of the `api.js` file to `networkNode.js`.

8. Now we're all set to run the `networkNode.js` file by passing in the variable of whatever port we want as a variable.

9. Let's run the `networkNode.js` file. In the terminal window, type `npm start`. By typing this command, the server should start listening to port `3001`, as we can observe in the following screenshot:

```
→ blockchain git:(master) npm start

> blockchain@1.0.0 start /Users/Eric/programs/blockchain
> nodemon --watch dev -e js dev/networkNode.js 3001


[nodemon] 1.17.3
[nodemon] to restart at any time, enter `rs`
[nodemon] watching: /Users/Eric/programs/blockchain/dev/**/*
[nodemon] starting `node dev/networkNode.js 3001`
Listening on port 3001...
```

10. From the preceding screenshot, we can observe that the server is listening to port `3001`. We can further verify this by typing `localhost:3001/blockchain` in the browser. You should see an output similar to what's shown in the following screenshot:

```
{
    "chain": [
        {
            "index": 1,
            "timestamp": 1524522321267,
            "transactions": [],
            "nonce": 100,
            "hash": "0",
            "previousBlockHash": "0"
        }
    ],
    "pendingTransactions": []
}
```

11. From the preceding screenshot, we can see that our blockchain is now hosted on port 3001 instead of on port 3000. If we went to port 3000, there would be nothing there, as shown in the following screenshot:

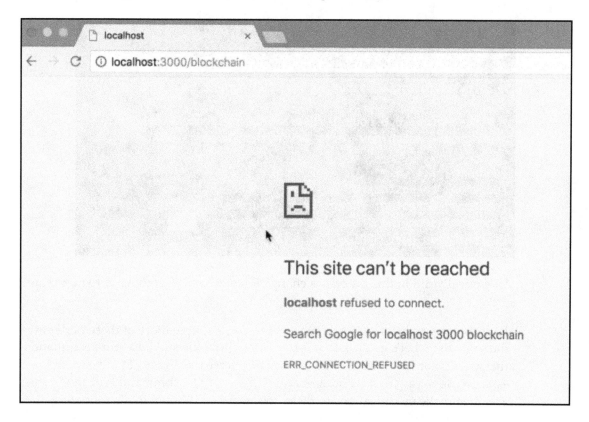

Running multiple instances of networkNode.js

The next thing that we will want to do is run multiple instances of networkNode.js. To do that, we are going to add a few more commands to the package.json file:

1. To begin with, in the package.json file, we must change the "start" command to "node_1". Now, when we run this command, it's going to start our first node, which is on port 3001. Let's give this a try.

2. Save the file, go to your terminal, and cancel the previous process by typing ^C%. After doing this, instead of typing `npm start`, type `npm run node_1`. With the help of this command, run our `node_1` on port `3001`:

```
^C%
→ blockchain git:(master) ✗
→ blockchain git:(master) ✗
→ blockchain git:(master) ✗ npm run node_1

> blockchain@1.0.0 node_1 /Users/Eric/programs/blockchain
> nodemon --watch dev -e js dev/networkNode.js 3001

[nodemon] 1.17.3
[nodemon] to restart at any time, enter `rs`
[nodemon] watching: /Users/Eric/programs/blockchain/dev/**/*
[nodemon] starting `node dev/networkNode.js 3001`
Listening on port 3001...
```

All we really did in this process is change the `npm start` command to `npm run node_1`.

3. For our decentralized network, we want to run a couple more of these nodes at the same time. Let's go back to our `package.json` file and add more commands that are similar to `"node_1"`. To do this, duplicate the `"node_1": "nodemon --watch dev -e js dev/networkNode.js 3001"`, command four more times and then make modifications to these commands, as shown in the following screenshot:

```
"node_1": "nodemon --watch dev -e js dev/networkNode.js 3001",
"node_2": "nodemon --watch dev -e js dev/networkNode.js 3002",
"node_3": "nodemon --watch dev -e js dev/networkNode.js 3003",
"node_4": "nodemon --watch dev -e js dev/networkNode.js 3004",
"node_5": "nodemon --watch dev -e js dev/networkNode.js 3005"
```

4. Now, save this modification and let's head back over to our terminal and start up the other network nodes. From the previous run, we have the first node, node_1, running on port 3001. For this run, we'll want to run the second node, node_2, on port 3002. Therefore, simply type npm   run node_2 and then press *Enter*. We'll get to observe the following output on the screen:

```
→ blockchain git:(master) ✗ npm run node_2

> blockchain@1.0.0 node_2 /Users/Eric/programs/blockchain
> nodemon --watch dev -e js dev/networkNode.js 3002


[nodemon] 1.17.3
[nodemon] to restart at any time, enter `rs`
[nodemon] watching: /Users/Eric/programs/blockchain/dev/**/*
[nodemon] starting `node dev/networkNode.js 3002`
Listening on port 3002...
```

We now have one network node running on port 3001, and the other network node running on port 3002. Follow a similar process to run the remaining network nodes on the remaining ports.

 For better visualization and easy understanding, it is recommended that you try to run each node on different tabs of the terminal window.

By following this process, what we are actually doing is creating five different instances of our networkNode.js file. So, essentially, we have five different network nodes running.

In the browser, we can check each one of these network nodes by changing the port number in localhost:3001/blockchain. By doing this, we're going to get back a different blockchain running on the different ports.

Testing the multiple nodes

We will continue exploring the five separate network nodes that we created in the previous section. By now, you might have all five of the network nodes running. If not, going to the previous section and understanding how to get each of these nodes running is recommended. What we've currently got, which is five separate network nodes running, is not really a network. All we have is five separate nodes or five separate instances of our API running, but they are not connected in any way. To verify that these network nodes are not connected, we can carry out a couple of tests:

1. So, let's head over to Postman and try make a couple of different transactions by hitting the /transaction endpoint on the different network nodes that we have running.

2. The first transaction that we want to make is going to be to our network node, which is hosted on port 3001. So, let's go into the body and type in some random transaction data, as shown in the following screenshot:

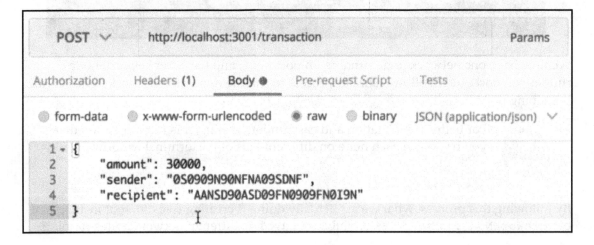

3. Our transaction data has an amount of 30,000 bitcoins, and we're sending this to network node that's hosted on port `3001`. Click on the **Send** button, and if the transaction is successful you'll get the following response, as highlighted in the following screenshot:

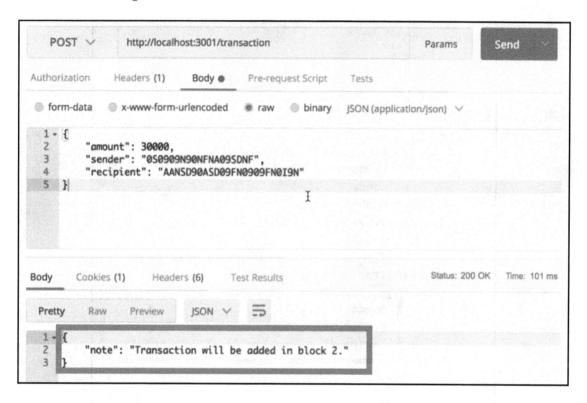

4. Now let's make a transaction to our network node hosted on port `3003` with the transaction amount as 10 bitcoins. Then click on the **Send** button to send the transaction to the network node on port `3003`. Here you will also get to observe the similar response.

5. Now that we have sent the transaction data to the network nodes, let's verify it. Go to the browser and go to `localhost:3001/blockchain`, and then press *Enter*. You'll get to observe a similar response, as shown in the following screenshot:

From the preceding screenshot, you can observe that we have one pending transaction for 30,000 bitcoin. That's one of the transactions that we just added.

6. Now, in the other tab, if we go to `localhost:3002/blockchain`, you'll see that we have no pending transactions because we did not send any transactions to this network node:

```
                    localhost:3001/blockchain    ×    localhost:3002/blockchain    ×

        ←    C    ⓘ localhost:3002/blockchain

        {
            "chain": [
                {
                    "index": 1,
                    "timestamp": 1524522573820,
                    "transactions": [],
                    "nonce": 100,
                    "hash": "0",
                    "previousBlockHash": "0"
                }
            ],
            "pendingTransactions": []
        }
```

7. Next, if we go to `localhost:3003/blockchain`, you'll see that we have a
    pending transaction here for the amount of 10 Bitcoin:

```
            localhost:3001/blockchain    ×    localhost:3002/blockchain    ×    localhost:3003/blockchain    ×

    ←    C    ⓘ localhost:3003/blockchain

    {
        "chain": [
            {
                "index": 1,
                "timestamp": 1524522617937,
                "transactions": [],
                "nonce": 100,
                "hash": "0",
                "previousBlockHash": "0"
            }
        ],
        "pendingTransactions": [
            {
                "amount": 10,
                "sender": "0S0909N90NFNA09SDNF",
                "recipient": "AANSD90ASD09FN0909FN0I9N"
            }
        ]
    }
```

This was one of the other transactions that we made.

If we were to go to `localhost: 3004/blockchain` and `localhost:3005/blockchain`, there should be no transactions there as we've not sent any of the transactions to these network nodes.

The conclusion that we can draw from this test is that although we do have five different network nodes running parallel to each other, they are not connected in any way. As a consequence, our main motive of this chapter will be to connect all of the network nodes to each other in order to build up a decentralized network.

Adding the currentNodeUrl

After testing our nodes, the next thing that we're going to do is alter the commands in our `package.json` slightly. The reason that we're going to do this is because we want each of our network nodes to be aware of what URL they are currently on. For example, they could be on `http://localhost:3001`, `localhost:3002`, `localhost:3003`, and so on. Therefore, we want each node to be aware of the URL that it is being hosted on.

In our `package.json`, as a third parameter to each of our commands, we are going to add the node's URL. Therefore, our first node's URL will simply be `http://localhost:3001`. It is likely that for our second node it will be `http://localhost:3002`. Similarly, you can add URLs for the remaining nodes, as shown in the following screenshot:

```
"nodemon --watch dev -e js dev/networkNode.js 3001 http://localhost:3001",
"nodemon --watch dev -e js dev/networkNode.js 3002 http://localhost:3002",
"nodemon --watch dev -e js dev/networkNode.js 3003 http://localhost:3003",
"nodemon --watch dev -e js dev/networkNode.js 3004 http://localhost:3004",
"nodemon --watch dev -e js dev/networkNode.js 3005 http://localhost:3005"
```

After adding the URLs, save the file. Now we have the URL of each node being passed in as an argument to the command we use to run each node. Therefore, we should have access to these URLs inside of our file, just like we have access to our port variables inside of our files.

Now let's go to the `blockchain.js` file, and at the part where we define the const, we're going to type the following:

```
const currentNodeUrl = process.argv[3];
```

With this command, we should have access to the current node's URL by using the `currentNodeUrl` variable.

Now we should assign the `currentNodeUrl` to our `Blockchain` data structure. We do this by typing the following highlighted line of code inside of our `function Blockchain {}`:

```
function Blockchain() {
        this.chain = [];
        this.pendingTransactions = [];

        this.currentNodeUrl = currentNodeUrl;
        this.createNewBlock();
};
```

Next, we also want our blockchain to be aware of all of the other nodes that are inside of our network. Therefore, we will add the following code below the preceding highlighted line of code:

```
this.networkNodes = [];
```

In the further sections, we'll fill up this array with the node URLs of all the other nodes in our network so that every node will be aware of all the other nodes inside of our blockchain network.

New endpoints outline

In our blockchain, we would now like to create a network and have a way to register all of the different nodes that we have with it. Therefore, let's make a couple more endpoints that will make it possible to register nodes with our network.

Defining the /register-and-broadcast-node endpoint

The first endpoint that we create will be `/register-and-broadcast-node`, and this is defined as follows:

```
app.post('/register-and-broadcast-node', function (req, res) {

});
```

The preceding endpoint will register a node and broadcast that node to the whole network. It will do this by passing the URL of the node we want to register on the `req` body. Therefore, type the following inside the preceding endpoint:

```
const newNodeUrl = req.body.newNodeUrl;
```

We're not going to build this endpoint now, but when we use it in later sections, we'll be sending in the URL of a new node that we want to add to our network. Then we're going to make some calculations and broadcast the node to the entire network so that all the other nodes can add it as well.

Creating the /register-node endpoint

The `/register-node` will be the next endpoint that we'll add to our network. This is defined as follows:

```
app.post('/register-node', function (req, res) {

});
```

This endpoint will register a node with the network.

The difference between register-and-broadcast-node and register-node endpoint

Now let's try to understand how the `/register-and-broadcast-node` and `/register-node` endpoints are different. Basically, what's going to happen here is that whenever we want to register a new node with our network, we are going to hit the `/register-and-broadcast-node` endpoint. This endpoint is going to register the new node on its own server, and then it's going to broadcast this new node to all of the other network nodes.

Those network nodes will simply accept the new network node inside of the `/register-node` endpoint, because all these nodes have to do is simply register the broadcast nodes. We just want them to register the new node; we do not want them to broadcast the new node because this has already occurred.

If all of the other nodes in the network were to broadcast the new node as well, that would severely degrade the performance of our blockchain network and would lead to an infinite loop that would crash our blockchain. Therefore, when all of the other network nodes receive the new node's URL, we just want them to register it and not broadcast it.

Defining the /register-nodes-bulk endpoint

The final endpoint that we're going to build in this section will be the `/register-nodes-bulk` endpoint:

```
app.post('/register-nodes-bulk', function (req, res) {

});
```

This endpoint will register multiple nodes at once.

Understanding how all of the endpoints work together

Learning about all of these endpoints might seem little bit confusing at this stage, so let's try to understand this with the help of a diagram. In the following diagram, we have our blockchain network:

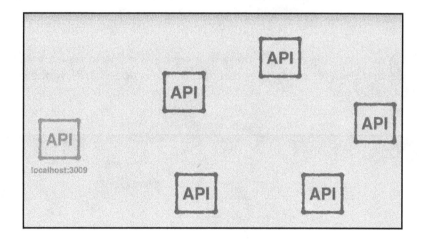

Now let's assume that these five network nodes are already connected to each other, thus forming our decentralized network. Also, let's assume that we want to add a node that is hosted on `localhost:3009` to our network.

The first thing that we'll do to add that node to our network is hit the `register-and-broadcast-node` endpoint on one of our network nodes:

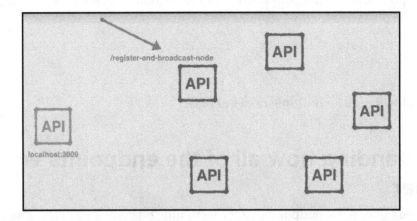

When we hit the `register-and-broadcast-node` endpoint, we need to send the URL of the new node that we want to add to our network. For our example, the URL is `localhost:3009`. This is the first step for adding a new node to our network. We have to hit our `register-and-broadcast-node` endpoint with the new nodes URL as data.

In the preceding diagram, the network node that we hit is going to register this new URL on its own node, and then it's going to broadcast this new node's URL to the rest of the network. All the other nodes in our network will receive this data at the `register-node` endpoint:

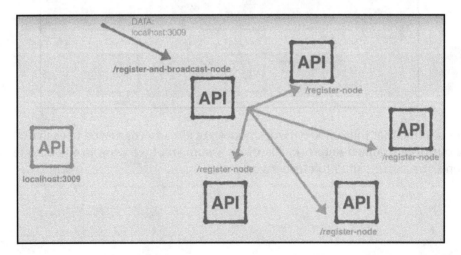

We're going to hit the `register-node` endpoint on all the other network nodes because we don't need to broadcast the data any more — we just need to register it.

Now, after the new URL is registered with all the other network nodes, our original node is going to make a request to the new node, and it's going to hit the `register-node-bulk` endpoint:

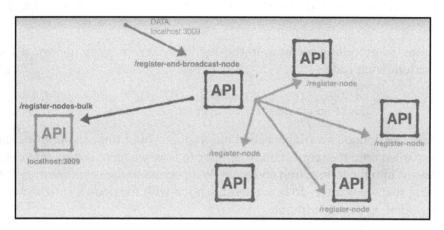

Furthermore, the original node is going to pass along the URLs of all the other nodes with it. So, this call will register all the other nodes that are already present inside of our network with the new node.

At this point, the node is now part of the network, and all of the nodes inside of the network will be aware of all the other nodes present in the network as well.

Now let's just go over the whole process one more time. The first thing that we're going to do to add a new node to our network is hit the `/register-and-broadcast-node` endpoint on one of the nodes inside of our network. This endpoint will register the new node's URL, and then it will broadcast that new URL to all the other nodes in the network. After the broadcast is complete, the original network node that we hit will send a request to the new network node and it will hit the `register-nodes-bulk` endpoint. In doing this, it will register all the other nodes in the network with our new node.

Consequently, when this whole process is complete, all of these nodes will be part of our decentralized blockchain network, and they will all be registered with each other.

This is how these three endpoints are going to work together. In the following section, we're going to build the `register-and-broadcast-node` endpoint.

Building the /register-and-broadcast-node endpoint

Let's start building our register and broadcast node endpoint. The function of this endpoint will be to register the new node with itself and then broadcast the new node to all the other nodes that are already present in the network. So, let's get started with building the endpoint:

1. From the preceding sections, in the `dev/networkNode.js` file, we already have the following code:

```
app.post('/register-and-broadcast-node', function(req, res) {
    const newNodeUrl = req.body.newNodeUrl;
```

Here, we defined a variable called `newNodeUrl`, and this `newNodeUrl` data will be passed onto the request body, similar to how we have transaction data being passed into the transaction endpoint. With access to the `newNodeUrl`, the first thing that we want to do is register the node with the node's `register-and-broadcast-node` endpoint.

2. To register it, all we have to do is put the `newNodeUrl` inside of our `networkNodes` array on our `blockchain` data structure. To do that, in the preceding code block, add the following highlighted code:

```
app.post('/register-and-broadcast-node', function(req, res) {
    const newNodeUrl = req.body.newNodeUrl;
    bitcoin.networkNodes.push(newNodeUrl);
```

3. By adding the preceding line of code, we are pushing the `newNodeUrl` into the `networkNodes` array. We only want to do this if the `newNodeUrl` isn't already present in the array. Check for this with the help of the `if` statement, as follows:

```
app.post('/register-and-broadcast-node', function(req, res) {
    const newNodeUrl = req.body.newNodeUrl;
    if (bitcoin.networkNodes.indexOf(newNodeUrl) == -1)
        bitcoin.networkNodes.push(newNodeUrl);
```

What the `if` statement is doing is checking if the `newNodeUrl` is not already present in the `networkNodes` array. If it is not present, then it is added to the array. Consequently, with the help of the preceding block of code, the `newNodeUrl` is registered with the `register-and-broadcast-node` endpoint.

4. Now that we've registered the `newNodeUrl`, what we have to do now is broadcast it to all the other nodes inside of the network. To do that, add the following line of code after the if block:

```
bitcoin.networkNodes.forEach(networkNodeUrl => {
    //... '/register-node'

}
```

In the preceding block of code, for each network node that is already present in the network or for every network node that is already present inside of the `networkNodes` array, we want to register our `newNodeUrl` with each of these `networkNodes` by hitting the register node endpoint. To do this, we're going to have to make a request to every single node at this endpoint.

5. We're going to make this request by importing a new library. Let's head over to the terminal to import the library. In the terminal, we're going to cancel our first network node and then type the following command:

```
npm install request-promise --save
```

6. Installing this `request-promise` library will allow us to make requests to all the other nodes in our network. Once the library has been installed, restart the first node again by typing `npm run node_1`.

7. Now let's go to the `dev/networkNode.js` file and import the library that we just downloaded to the code. Import the library by typing the following line of code at the start:

```
const rp = require('request-promise');
```

In the preceding line of code, `rp` stands for the request promise.

8. Now let's use this library in the `register-and-broadcast-node` endpoint. Over here, we have to broadcast our `newNodeUrl` to all the other nodes in our network. Do this with the help of the `request-promise` library that we just imported.

The next couple of steps that we are going to add to the code might look a little bit confusing as we're going through them, but don't worry. After the steps are complete, we'll walk through the code step by step to make sure that everything is clear to you. Now let's take a look at the following steps:

1. The first thing that we want to do for our `request-promise` library is define some options that we're going to use, so type in the following highlighted lines of code:

```
bitcoin.networkNodes.forEach(networkNodeUrl => {
    const requestOptions = {
    }

}
```

2. Inside of this object, we want to define the options that we want to use for each request.

3. The first option that we want to define is what URI/URL we want to hit. We know that we want to hit the `register-node` endpoints on all of our other `networkNodeUrl`. Consequently, we will add the following highlighted line of code to our preceding block:

```
bitcoin.networkNodes.forEach(networkNodeUrl => {
    const requestOptions = {
    uri: networkNodeUrl + '/register-node',
    }

}
```

4. Next, we want to define the method that we want to use. To hit the `register-node` endpoint, we'll have to use the `POST` method, so add the following code to the preceding code block:

```
method: 'POST',
```

5. Then we want to find out what data we're going to pass along with this request, so add the following:

```
body: { newNodeUrl: newNodeUrl }
```

6. Finally, we're going to set the `json` option to true so that we can send it as JSON data:

```
json: true
```

7. These are the options that we want to use for each request we make. Now let's see how we can use these options. After the `requestOptions` block, add the following line of code:

```
rp(requestOptions)
```

8. The preceding request is going to return a promise to us, and we want to get all of these promises back in a single array. So, before and inside of the `forEach` loop, carry out the following highlighted changes:

```
const regNodesPromises = [];
bitcoin.networkNodes.forEach(networkNodeUrl => {
    const requestOptions = {
        uri: networkNodeUrl + '/transaction',
        method: 'POST',
        body: newTransaction,
        json: true
    };
    regNodesPromises.push(rp(requestOptions));
});
```

9. Now, outside of the `forEach` loop, we want to run all of the promises that we had requested. Add the following code after the loop:

```
Promise.all(regNodesPromises)
.then(data => {
    //use the data...
});
```

Continuing to work on the /register-and-broadcast-node endpoint

In this section, let's continue to build our `register-and-broadcast-node` endpoint. So far, we have registered the new node with the current network node that we're on and we have broadcast the new node to all the other nodes in our network. Consequently, we're hitting the `register-node` endpoint on all the other nodes inside of our network. Also, for now, we're assuming that those other nodes are registering the new node, which we haven't built yet, but we're assuming that it's working.

After the whole broadcast is completed, we must register all of the nodes that are currently inside of our network with the one new node that we are adding to the network. For that, we're going to use our `request-promise` library. Therefore, we need to define some options, as highlighted in the following code:

```
Promise.all(regNodesPromises)
.then(data => {
    const bulkRegisterOptions = {
        uri: newNodeUrl + '/register-nodes-bulk'
        method: 'POST',
```

```
        body: {allNetworkNodes: [...bitcoin.networkNodes,
        bitcoin.currentNodeUrl]}
        json:true
    };
  });
});
```

In the preceding code, the options that we want to use (such as `uri`) are defined, along with the `POST` method. In the body option, we defined the `allNetworkNodes` array, and inside of this array, we want all of the URLs of all the nodes in our network, plus the URL of the node that we're currently on. Furthermore, you might have noticed that we used a spread operator `...` in the array because `bitcoin.networkNodes` is an array and we don't want one inside of another. Instead, we want to spread out all the elements of this array and put them inside of our outer array. Finally, we want to define `json` as being `true`.

Next, we want to make the request, so after the options block, add the following:

```
return rp(bulkRegisterOptions);
```

After this, add the following:

```
.then (data => {

})
```

The `data` variable present in the preceding line of code will actually be the data that we receive from the aforementioned promise. We're not going to do anything with this data, but we want to use `.then` because we want to do the next step inside of our endpoint. However, we can only do this after the aforementioned promise has completed.

The last step that we must complete inside of this endpoint is send a response back to whoever called it. Therefore, type the following highlighted lines of code:

```
.then (data => {
    res.json({ note: 'New Node registered with network successfully' });
});
```

That is it for our `register-and-broadcast-node` endpoint.

A quick recap of how the register-and-broadcast-node endpoint functions

Now let's run through this endpoint again for a quick summary of what we did in this endpoint so that we have a better understanding of this. Whenever we want to register a new node with our network, the `register-and-broadcast-node` endpoint is the first point that we want to hit. The first thing that we're doing inside of this endpoint is taking the `newNodeUrl` and registering it with the current node by pushing it into our `networkNodes` array.

The next step that we have to make is to broadcast this `newNodeUrl` to the rest of the nodes in our network. We are doing that inside of the `forEach` loop. All that's happening inside of this for loop is we're making a request to each of the other nodes in our network. We're making this request to the `register-node` endpoint. We are then pushing all of these requests into our `register-node` promises array, and then we're simply running all of those requests.

Once all of these requests are completed without any errors, we can assume that the `newNodeUrl` has been registered successfully with all of our other network nodes.

After our broadcast is complete, the next thing that we want to do is register all of the network nodes that are already present inside of our network with our new node. To do this, we make a single request to our new node and we hit the `register-nodes-bulk` endpoint. The data that we pass along to this endpoint is the URLs of all the nodes that are already present inside of our network.

We then run `rp(bulkRegisterOptions);`, and even though we haven't built the `register-nodes-bulk` endpoint yet, we're going to assume that it's working and that all of our network nodes have been registered with our new nodes successfully. Once that has happened, all of our calculations are complete, and we simply send back a note saying that the new node has been registered with the network successfully.

This may seem like a lot to take in at this point, but don't worry; it is recommended that you continue moving forward. In further sections, we're going to build our `register-node` endpoint, followed by our `register-nodes-bulk` endpoint. As we do this, everything should become clearer to you.

Building the /register-node endpoint

Now that we have built the `/register-and-broadcast-node` endpoint, it's time we move on to some things that are a little less complex. In this section, let's begin building the `register-node` endpoint. This is going to be very straightforward compared to the endpoint that we built in the previous section.

This `register-node` endpoint is where every node in the network is going to receive the broadcast that is sent out by our `register-and-broadcast-node` endpoint. The only thing that this `register-node` endpoint has to do is register the new node with the node that receives the request for it.

To begin building the `register-node` endpoint, follow these steps:

1. The first thing that we'll have to do is define the `newNodeUrl`; therefore, add the following highlighted line of code:

```
// register a node with the network
app.post('/register-node', function(req, res) {
        const newNodeUrl = req.body.newNodeUrl;
});
```

The preceding line of code is simply stating to use the value of `newNodeUrl` that is sent to `req.body`. This is the data that we send to the `/register-node` endpoint, and we're going to save that new `nodeNodeUrl` as the `newNodeUrl` variable.

2. Next, we want to register the `newNodeUrl` variable with the node that received the request. To do that, add the following highlighted line of code:

```
// register a node with the network
app.post('/register-node', function(req, res) {
        const newNodeUrl = req.body.newNodeUrl;
        bitcoin.networkNodes.push(newNodeUrl);
});
```

The preceding line of code will register our new node with the node that we are currently on. All we'll do here is simply push the `newNodeUrl` into the current node's `networkNodes` array.

3. Now, the final thing that we have to do is send back a response, so type the following highlighted line of code:

```
// register a node with the network
app.post('/register-node', function(req, res) {
        const newNodeUrl = req.body.newNodeUrl;
        bitcoin.networkNodes.push(newNodeUrl);
        res.json({ note: 'New node registered successfully.' });
});
```

4. Next, we want to do some error handling inside of this endpoint. The only thing that we want to do is add `newNodeUrl` to our `networkNodes` array, if it doesn't already exist in that array. To do this, we are going to add an if statement at the start of `bitcoin.networkNodes.push(newNodeUrl)`. But before that, let's define a variable, as follows:

```
// register a node with the network
app.post('/register-node', function(req, res) {
        const newNodeUrl = req.body.newNodeUrl;
        const nodeNotAlreadyPresent =
          bitcoin.networkNodes.indexOf(newNodeUrl) == -1;
        bitcoin.networkNodes.push(newNodeUrl);
        res.json({ note: 'New node registered successfully.' });
});
```

What this preceding highlighted line is stating is that if the index of the `newNodeUrl` is negative 1, or, in other words, if the `newNodeUrl` does not exist in our network nodes, then the `nodeNotAlreadyPresent` variable will be true. If the `newNodeUrl` already exists in our `networkNodes` array, then this variable will be false.

5. Inside of the if statement, what we're going to state is that if the `newNodeUrl` is not present in our `networkNodes` array then add it by running `bitcoin.networkNodes.push(newNodeUrl)`:

```
if (nodeNotAlreadyPresent ) bitcoin.networkNodes.push(newNodeUrl);
```

6. Next, there's one other case that we want to handle, which is that we do not want to push the `newNodeUrl` into our `networkNodes` array if the `newNodeUrl` is actually the URL of the current node that we're on. To mention this condition in the code, let's first have to define a variable:

```
const notCurrentNode = bitcoin.currentNodeUrl !== newNodeUrl;
```

The preceding line is simply evaluating the `bitcoin.currentNodeUrl !==` `newNodeUrl` expression, which states whether or not the `currentNodeUrl` equals the `newNodeUrl`. If not, then the `notCurrentNode` variable will be true. If they do equal each other, then the variable will be false.

7. Next, we just want to add the `notCurrentNode` variable to our if statement, as follows:

```
if (nodeNotAlreadyPresent && notCurrentNode )
bitcoin.networkNodes.push(newNodeUrl);
```

What's happening in this if statement is that if the new node is not already present in our `networkNodes` array and if the new node is not the same URL as the current node that we're on, then we just want to add the new node to our `networkNodes` array.

Everything that we have learned here is error handling inside of the endpoint.

Testing the /register-node endpoint

In this section, let's test the `/register-node` endpoint to make sure that it works properly and to get a better understanding of how it works.

Installing the request library

Before we get into testing the endpoint, there is a small update that we need to carry out. The update is regarding installing the request library. A few sections prior, we installed the `request-promise` library. Now, to test the endpoints that we just created, it might be necessary for us to also install the request library, depending on what version of the `request-promise` library we have.

To install the request library, simply go to your terminal, and inside of the `blockchain` directory run the following command:

```
npm install request --save
```

Endpoint testing

Before we get into testing, check whether you have all five of our network nodes running inside of your terminal. If not, then you will have to set them up. Let's test the `register-node` endpoint by using Postman:

1. To start with, we're going to type `http://localhost:3001/register-node` in the address bar, as shown in the following screenshot:

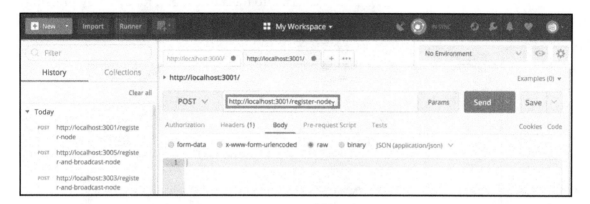

   When we hit this endpoint, we are expected to send in a `newNodeUrl` as data on our `req.body`. We'll have to set that up now. So, in the **Body** tab inside of the Postman, we want to have **raw** selected and **JSON (application/json)** selected as the text.

2. Then, inside the textbox, make an object and add the following code:

```
{
    "newNodeUrl":""
}
```

3. Now let's say that we want to register our node that is running on port 3002 with our node that's running on port 3001. Add the following to our preceding code:

```
{
    "newNodeUrl":"http://localhost:3002"
}
```

   So far, we have registered our node that's running on `localhost:3002` with our node that's running on `localhost:3001`. Therefore, when we hit `http://localhost:3001/register-node`, our `localhost:3002` should show up in the `networkNodes` array of our first node (that is, `localhost:3001`) because this `register-node` endpoint registers a node by placing it into the `networkNodes` array.

4. To verify this, go to Postman and click on the **Send** button. You will get the response **New node registered successfully**. Now go over to your browser and type `localhost:3001/blockchain` into the address bar, followed by pressing *Enter*. You will see an output similar to what's shown in the following screenshot:

Since we had just registered our second node with our current node on `localhost:3001`, we have our second node's URL inside of this array.

Following the same procedure, you can try to register other nodes too. Try experimenting with this. This will help you in gaining a clear understanding of the nodes that are registered. If you come across any issues, try to read through the whole procedure again.

One important thing that we want to notice here is that if we now go to `localhost:3002/blockchain`, we get to observe that there are no network nodes registered in the `networkNodes` array.

Ideally, what we want to happen is that when we register a new node, we want it to reverse register as well. So, if we register `localhost:3002` with the node on `3001`, then our node on `3002` should register `localhost:3001`. That way, both of these nodes will be aware of each other.

We've actually already built this functionality inside of our `register-and-broadcast-node` endpoint. Once we build all three of these endpoints, the functionality that we mentioned will work properly.

Building the /register-nodes-bulk endpoint

The next endpoint that we are going to build is our `register-nodes-bulk` endpoint; this is the final endpoint that we need to build. These three endpoints that we have been working on will all work together to create our decentralized blockchain network.

Before we start building the endpoint, let's try to understand what the `register-nodes-bulk` endpoint does. Whenever a new node gets broadcast to all the other nodes inside of the network, we want to take all of the nodes that are already inside of the network and send that data back to our new node so that the new node can register and recognize all of the nodes that are already present inside of the network.

The `register-nodes-bulk` endpoint will be accepting data that contains the URLs of every node that is already present in the network. Then, we're simply going to register all of these network nodes with the new node.

The new node is the node on which the `register-nodes-bulk` endpoint is hit. This endpoint is only ever hit on a new node that's being added to our network.

1. To build the `register-nodes-bulk` endpoint, we'll have to make an assumption that all of the node URLs that are currently in our network are being passed in as data, and that we can access them on the `req.body.allNetworkNodes` property. This is because we're sending in the `allNetworkNodes` data when we call this endpoint in the `Promise.all(regNodesPromise)` block. Over here, we're sending in `allNetworkNodes` to the `register-nodes-bulk` endpoint. This will give us access to the `allNetworkNodes` data inside of the endpoint.

2. Let's add the following line of code to our `register-nodes-bulk` endpoint that we created in the previous sections:

```
app.post('/register-nodes-bulk', function (req, res) {
    const allNetworkNodes = req.body.allNetowrkNodes;

});
```

3. Next, let's loop through every node URL present in the `allNetworkNodes` array and register it with the new node, as follows:

```
app.post('/register-nodes-bulk', function (req, res) {
    const allNetworkNodes = req.body.allNetowrkNodes;
    allNetworkNodes.forEach(networkNodeUrl => {
        //...
    });

});
```

4. Now, all we're going to do inside of the loop is register each network node URL with the current node that we're on, which is the new node being added to the network:

```
app.post('/register-nodes-bulk', function (req, res) {
    const allNetworkNodes = req.body.allNetowrkNodes;
    allNetworkNodes.forEach(networkNodeUrl => {
        bitcoin.networkNodes.push(metworkNodeUrl);
    });

});
```

What's happening in the preceding highlighted line of code is that as we cycle through all the network nodes with our `forEach` loop, we are registering each one by pushing that `networkNodeUrl` into our `networkNodes` array.

Whenever we hit the `/register-nodes-bulk` endpoint, we are on the new node that's being added to the network. All of these `networkNodeUrls` are being registered to the new node that we are adding.

5. Now there are a couple of instances in which we do not want to add a `networkNodeUrl` to our `networkNodes` array. To handle these instances, we are going to use an if statement. But before that, we need to define a conditional statement, as follows:

```
const nodeNotAlreadyPresent =
bitcoin.networkNodes.indexOf(networkNodeUrl) == -1;
```

One reason that we would not want to add a `networkNodeUrl` to our `networkNodes` array is if this `networkNodeUrl` already exists in our `networkNodes` array; that's what we have mentioned in the conditional statement.

All this statement is doing is testing to see if the `networkNodeUrl` that we're on is present inside of our `networkNodes` array. From here, it will simply evaluate this as either true or false.

6. Now we can add the `nodeNotAlreadyPresent` variable and the if statement, as highlighted in the following code :

```
app.post('/register-nodes-bulk', function (req, res) {
    const allNetworkNodes = req.body.allNetowrkNodes;
    allNetworkNodes.forEach(networkNodeUrl => {
    const nodeNotAlreadyPresent =
      bitcoin.networkNodes.indexOf(networkNodeUrl) == -1;
    if(nodeNotAlreadyPresent)bitcoin.networkNodes.push(networkNodeUrl);
    });

});
```

The preceding if statement states that if the node is not already present inside of our `networkNodes` array, then we're going to register that node.

7. Now, another instance in which we would not want to register a network node is if that network node has the same URL as the network node that we are currently on. To handle this, we'll have to make another variable:

```
const notCurrentNode = bitcoin.currentNodeUrl !==networkNodeUrl
```

8. Next, add this variable to our `if` statement:

```
app.post('/register-nodes-bulk', function (req, res) {
    const allNetworkNodes = req.body.allNetowrkNodes;
    allNetworkNodes.forEach(networkNodeUrl => {
    const nodeNotAlreadyPresent =
      bitcoin.networkNodes.indexOf(networkNodeUrl) == -1;
        if(nodeNotAlreadyPresent && notCurrentNode)
          bitcoin.networkNodes.push(networkNodeUrl);
    });

});
```

Basically, all we're stating in the `if` statement is that as we cycle through each network node that we're adding, if that node is not already present in our network node array and if that node is not our current node's URL, then we want to add the `networkNodeUrl` to our `networkNodes` array.

9. Once we have completed the `forEach` loop, we'll have registered all of the network nodes that are already present inside of our blockchain network. All we have to do at this point is send back a response, as follows:

```
app.post('/register-nodes-bulk', function (req, res) {
    const allNetworkNodes = req.body.allNetowrkNodes;
    allNetworkNodes.forEach(networkNodeUrl => {
    const nodeNotAlreadyPresent =
      bitcoin.networkNodes.indexOf(networkNodeUrl) == -1;
        if(nodeNotAlreadyPresent && notCurrentNode)
          bitcoin.networkNodes.push(networkNodeUrl);
  });
    res.json({note: 'Bulk registration successful.' });

  });
```

Let's quickly review what we have done so far. The endpoint that we've built is accepting all of the network nodes as data, and then we are cycling through all of the network nodes that are already present in our blockchain network. For each node, as long as it is not already registered with the `currentNode` and is not the same URL as the `currentNode`, we are going to add the node to our `networkNodes` array.

Testing the /register-nodes-bulk endpoint

In this section, we're going to test our `register-nodes-bulk` endpoint to make sure that it works properly. This will allow us to gain a clear understanding of how it works:

1. To test the endpoint, we are going to head over to Postman. Here, we'll hit the `localhost:3001/register-nodes-bulk` endpoint. When we test this endpoint, we expect to receive some data, which is the `allNetworkNodes` array.

2. Consequently, in the body tab inside Postman, with the **raw** option and **JSON (application/json)** format selected for the text, add the following lines of code to the body:

```
{
    "allNetworkNodes": []
}
```

3. Inside of this array, there are going to be the URLs of all of the nodes that are already present in our blockchain network:

```
{
    "allNetworkNodes": [
    "http://localhost:3002",
    "http://localhost:3003",
    "http://localhost:3004"
    ]
}
```

4. When we run this request now, we should register all three of these URLs with our node that's running on `localhost:3001`. Let's see if that works. Click on the **Send** button and you will receive a response that states **Bulk registration successful.**

5. Now, if we head over to the browser, we can double check that it worked. In the address bar, type `localhost:3001/blockchain` and then press *Enter*. You will get to observe the three URLs that were added inside of `networkNodes` array, since those are bulk registered:

Similarly, you can try experimenting by adding new nodes to the other nodes on different URLs. You'll get to observe the similar response in the `networkNodes` array of these nodes.

So, it looks like our `register-node-bulk` endpoint is working just as it should.

Testing all of the network endpoints

From what we have learned in the preceding section, we know that our `register-node` route and that the `register-nodes-bulk` route are both working correctly. So, in this section, let's put it all together and test our `register-and-broadcast-node` route, which uses the both the `register-node` route and the `register-nodes-bulk` route.

The `register-and-broadcast-node` endpoint will allow us to build a decentralized blockchain network by allowing us to create a network and add new nodes to it. Let's jump right into our first example to get a better understanding of it. To understand how the `register-and-broadcast-node` route works, we'll make use of Postman.

In the Postman application, we want to make a post request to register and broadcast the node on `localhost:3001`. However, before we do that, just make sure that all four nodes are running so that we can test the routes.

At this point, we have no network at all; we just have five individual nodes running, but they are not connected in any way. Therefore, the first call that we're going to make is simply going to connect two nodes together to form the beginnings of our network. We will now register a node with our node that's hosted on port `3001`. When we hit the `register-and-broadcast-node` endpoint, we must send in a `newNodeUrl` that we want to register. In Postman, add the following code:

```
{
    "newNodeUrl": ""
}
```

For this first test, we want to register our second node hosted on port `3002` with our first node. To do that, we will add the following highlighted code:

```
{
    "newNodeUrl": "http://localhost:3002"
}
```

Now, when we make this request, it should register our node that's hosted on `localhost:3002` with our node that's hosted on `localhost:3001`. Let's verify this by clicking the **Send** button. You will see an output similar to what's shown in the following screenshot:

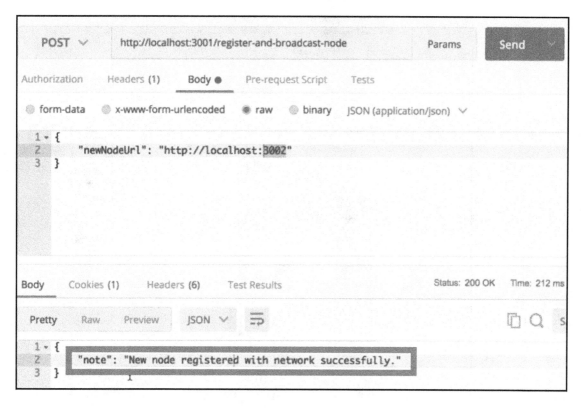

From the preceding screenshot, we can see that the new node has been registered successfully with the network. Let's verify this by going to the browser.

In the browser, you will have access to all five nodes that are running. We have now registered the node on port `3002` with the node hosted on `localhost:3001`. So, if we refresh the page on the browser now, we'll get to observe that `localhost:3002` has been registered in the `networkNodes` array of port `3001`:

From the preceding screenshot, we can see that we've registered `localhost:3002`. Now, if we go to `localhost:3002`, we should have `localhost:3001` registered in its `networkNodes` array. Let's refresh and see what we get here:

From the preceding screenshot, we can see that both nodes have now formed a network and registered each other as a network node.

Next, let's add another node to this network. Let's head back to Postman and change the localhost:3002 to localhost:3003. We're going to make a request to the node that is on 3001:

```
{
    "newNodeUrl": "http://localhost:3003"
}
```

What this should do is register our node that's hosted on `localhost:3003` with all the other nodes in the network. So, `3003` should register with `3001` and `3002`. Let's send this request and see if it works. If it's successfully registered, you will see an output similar to what's shown in the following screenshot:

Let's verify this in our browser. When we refresh in the `localhost:3001`, we should have `localhost: 3003` inside of the `networkNodes` array:

Now, since `localhost:3002` is also part of the network, it should have `localhost:3003` inside of the `networkNodes` array. When we made this request, we made it to `3001` not `3002`. Localhost `3002` was already part of the network, and the broadcast registered `3003` with all the network nodes that are present in the network. To verify this, refresh the `networkNodes` array on `3002`. You will see an output similar to what's shown in the following screenshot:

From the preceding screenshot, we can see that we have our third node inside of the `localhost:3002 networkNodes` array as well now. Furthermore, if we go over to the `networkNodes` on `localhost:3003` and refresh the page, we should have both `3001` and `3002` inside of the `networkNodes` array:

```
{
    "chain": [
        {
            "index": 1,
            "timestamp": 1524778518209,
            "transactions": [],
            "nonce": 100,
            "hash": "0",
            "previousBlockHash": "0"
        }
    ],
    "pendingTransactions": [],
    "currentNodeUrl": "http://localhost:3003",
    "networkNodes": [
        "http://localhost:3002",
        "http://localhost:3001"
    ]
}
```

Consequently, we now have a network comprised of our nodes on `3001`, `3002`, and `3003`. These are registered with each other.

Now, let's head back to Postman and register the remaining `localhost:3004` and `localhost:3005` with the network by following the same procedures that we followed to register the initial nodes.

After registering both `3004` and `3005` with the network, if you go to the browser, all of these registered nodes should have `localhost:3004` and `localhost:3005` inside of their `networkNodes` array. Refresh the `localhost:3001` page and you see an output similar to what's shown in the following screenshot:

```
{
    "chain": [
        {
            "index": 1,
            "timestamp": 1524778518286,
            "transactions": [],
            "nonce": 100,
            "hash": "0",
            "previousBlockHash": "0"
        }
    ],
    "pendingTransactions": [],
    "currentNodeUrl": "http://localhost:3001",
    "networkNodes": [
        "http://localhost:3002",
        "http://localhost:3003",
        "http://localhost:3005",
        "http://localhost:3004"
    ]
}
```

Similarly, if you refresh the other pages, you will get to observe all the nodes, similar to what we observed in the preceding screenshot.

So, this is how we've built up a decentralized network that is comprised of five different nodes.

Now, you might be wondering how all of this is working. It's working because when we make a `"newNodeUrl": "http://localhost:3004"` request, we are actually adding a command to add `3004` to the network. But then how does `localhost:3004` become aware of the entire network from one request?

If you remember from the preceding sections, when we built the `/register-and-broadcast-node` endpoint, there was actually a lot of calculations going on. So, if we take a look at the `/register-and-broadcast-node` endpoint code, we can see that the first thing that happens inside of our `register-and-broadcast-node` endpoint is that we take in the `newNodeUrl` and then broadcast it to every single node in the network by hitting their `register-node` endpoint. So, every node in the network will become aware of the new node that's being added.

 For the complete code, please visit `https://github.com/PacktPublishing/Learn-Blockchain-Programming-with-JavaScript/blob/master/dev/networkNode.js` and refer to the code block which starts with this comment: `//registering a node and broadcasting it the network`.

Then, after the broadcast takes place, we send the request to the new node that was just added and register all of the network nodes that are already present in the network with the new node. This is where the reverse registration takes place. At this point, all of the original nodes in the network are aware of the new node, and the new node is aware of all the other nodes in the network. Thus, all of the nodes inside of the network become aware of each other, which is what needs to happen for our blockchain to work properly.

So, all three of the endpoints (`register-and-broadcast-node`, `register-node`, and `register-nodes-bulk`) that we built are very powerful because they work together to create a decentralized blockchain network. This is what we have built in this chapter.

At this point in the book, it is recommended that you to take some time to play around with these endpoints a little bit, making different networks with different nodes, and testing it a little bit more to get more familiar with how it's all working.

If you are confused about any of the concepts or topics we've covered, it is recommend that you once again read through all of the sections in this chapter. You'd be surprised how much you can learn and pick up the second time around after you already have some context for what is going to be happening and what we're going to be building.

Summary

We have now finished creating our decentralized network. In this chapter, we learned about a lot of new concepts. We began our journey by learning about how to create the multiple instances of our API and how to use them to set up our decentralized network. We then defined various endpoints such as `register-and-broadcast-node`, `register-node`, and `register-nodes-bulk`. After this, we built these endpoints and tested them.

In the next chapter, we will learn how to synchronize the network.

5
Synchronizing the Network

In the previous chapters, we built a network that was made up of five nodes. Every node was aware of all the other nodes in the network, which created a decentralized blockchain network. We now need to create a synchronized network, so that the blockchain on every node is the same and data is consistent throughout. We can't afford to have different versions of the blockchains running on different nodes, because this would totally destroy the purpose of having a blockchain. There should only be one version of the blockchain that is consistent across every node. Therefore, in this chapter, let's synchronize the network that we built in Chapter 4, *Creating a Decentralized Blockchain Network*. We'll do this by broadcasting transactions and new blocks that have been mined across all the nodes in the network.

In this chapter, the following topics will be covered:

- Understanding the need to synchronize the network
- Building the /transaction/broadcast endpoint
- Refactoring the createTransaction method and the /transaction endpoint
- Testing the transaction endpoints
- Updating the mining information
- Building the /receive-new-block endpoint
- Testing the new and updated /mine endpoints

Let's get started with synchronizing the network.

Understanding the need to synchronize the network

Let's try to understand why the network needs to be synchronized. We currently have a decentralized blockchain network that consists of five nodes. The data across these nodes is not consistent; data on each node might vary, which would lead to the failure of the purpose of having a blockchain. Let's try to understand this situation with the help of an example. Go to Postman and send a sample transaction, as shown in the following screenshot:

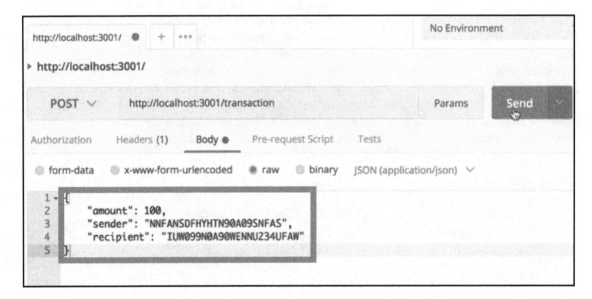

Send this transaction to the node that's hosted on `localhost:3001` by clicking on the **Send** button. This transaction will appear in the `pendingTransactions` array of `localhost:3001/blockchain`, which you can observe in the following screenshot:

```
{
    "chain": [
        {
            "index": 1,
            "timestamp": 1524846662704,
            "transactions": [],
            "nonce": 100,
            "hash": "0",
            "previousBlockHash": "0"
        }
    ],
    "pendingTransactions": [
        {
            "amount": 100,
            "sender": "NNFANSDFHYHTN90A09SNFAS",
            "recipient": "IUW099N0A90WENNU234UFAW"
        }
    ],
    "currentNodeUrl": "http://localhost:3001",
    "networkNodes": [
        "http://localhost:3002",
        "http://localhost:3003",
        "http://localhost:3004",
        "http://localhost:3005"
    ]
}
```

Now, go to any of the other nodes and check for the transactions that were sent. We won't be able to view the transactions in the pendingTransactions array on those nodes. The sample transaction that is sent will only be present in the node on localhost:3001. It isn't broadcast to any other nodes in the network.

What you are going to do in this chapter is to refactor the /transaction endpoint, so that whenever a transaction is created, it is broadcast to all nodes. This means that all nodes will have the same data. We need to do the same thing in order to mine a block. Let's refactor the /mine endpoint so that whenever a new block is mined, it is also broadcast throughout the entire network. This means that the entire network is synchronized and has the exact same number of blocks. Having data synchronized through the network is an important feature of blockchain technology.

Refactoring the createNewTransaction method and the /transaction endpoint

In this section, let's refactor the createNewTransaction method by splitting it into two separate parts. One part will simply create a new transaction and then return that transaction, and the other part will push the new transaction into the pendingTransactions array. We'll do the latter part by creating a separate method for it. We also create a new transaction endpoint called /transaction/broadcast. This endpoint will allow us to broadcast transactions throughout the entire blockchain network, so that every node has the same data and so that the entire network is synchronized.

Modifications to the createNewTransaction method

Here, let's split up the createNewTransaction method into two separate methods, by modifying it as follows:

1. Go to the createNewTransaction method in your dev/blockchain.js file. We built this method in Chapter 2, *Building a Blockchain* in the *Creating createNewTransaction method* section. For reference, take a look at the following createNewTransaction method:

```
Blockchain.prototype.createNewTransaction = function (amount,
sender, recipient) {
    const newTransaction = {
        amount: amount,
        sender: sender,
        recipient: recipient,
    };
    this.newTransactions.push(newTransaction);
```

```
        return.this.getlastBlock() ['index'] + 1;
    }
```

2. Let's make the following highlighted modifications to the method:

```
    Blockchain.prototype.createNewTransaction = function (amount,
    sender, recipient) {
        const newTransaction = {
            amount: amount,
            sender: sender,
            recipient: recipient,
            transactionId: uuid().split('-').join('')
        };
        return newTransaction;
    }
```

Here, an ID is added to every transaction. To create this ID, a unique string is used, which is very similar to what we had used for creating the node addresses in Chapter 3, *Accessing the Blockchain through an API*.

3. Unique strings for the IDs are created with the use of the uuid library. Therefore, at the start of the dev/blockchain.js file, where all the constants are defined, you need to add the following line of code in order to use the uuid library in our project:

```
    const uuid = require('uuid/v1');
```

In the modified method, you can observe that the following line of code was added to create unique strings for the transactionId values. This is where the use of the uuid library was implemented:

```
    transactionId: uuid().split('-').join('')
```

Here, the .split() function will take out the dashes that are added to the unique string, and then, the .join() function will rejoin the string to give an output of a unique Id for each transaction.

Building the addTransactionToPendingTransactions method

Next, we need to push the newTransaction that was returned to the pendingTransactions array of the blockchain. Therefore, let's create another method, called addTransactionToPendingTransactions:

1. In the dev/blockchain.js file, the addTransactionToPendingTransactions method will be defined as follows:

   ```
   Blockchain.prototype.addTransactionToPendingTransactions =
   function(transactionObj) {
   };
   ```

2. Next, take the transactionObj and push it to the pendingTransactions array of the blockchain:

   ```
   Blockchain.prototype.addTransactionToPendingTransaction =
   function(transactionObj) {
       this.pendingTransactions.push(transactionObj);

   };
   ```

3. Then, we simply want to return the index of the block to which the transaction is added:

   ```
   Blockchain.prototype.addTransactionToPendingTransaction =
   function(transactionObj) {
       this.pendingTransaction.push(transactionObj);
       return this.getLastBlock()['index'] + 1;
   };
   ```

To recap quickly, we modified the createNewTransaction method which creates a new transaction, and returns that new transaction. We then created a new method, called addTransactionToPendingTransactions. This method takes in a transactionObj and adds it to the pendingTransactions array on the blockchain. After that, we simply returned the index of the block to which the new transaction was added.

Building the /transaction/broadcast endpoint

In this section, let's build a new endpoint called /transaction/broadcast. Anytime we want to create a new transaction from now on, we're going to hit this /transaction/broadcast endpoint. This endpoint will do two things:

- It will create a new transaction.
- It will then broadcast that new transaction to all the other nodes in the network.

Let's go through the following steps to create the endpoint:

1. To add this endpoint, go to the dev/networkNode.js file where we have defined all the endpoints, and add this new endpoint as follows:

   ```
   app.post('/transaction/broadcast', function(req, res) ) {

   });
   ```

2. Then, in order for the endpoint to carry out the aforementioned functionalities, add the following highlighted code to the endpoint:

   ```
   app.post('/transaction/broadcast', function(req, res) ) {
       const newTransaction = bitcoin.createNewTransaction();

   });
   ```

   The createNewTransaction() method here is the modified method from the previous section.

3. The createNewTransaction() method takes in the amount, sender, and recipient parameters. For our endpoint, let's assume that all of that data is being sent on the req.body. Therefore, those parameters will be defined as shown highlighted in the following code:

   ```
   app.post('/transaction/broadcast', function(req, res) ) {
       const newTransaction =
   bitcoin.createNewTransaction(req.body.amount, req.body.sender,
   req.body.recipient);

   });
   ```

4. Next, let's add the `newTransaction` variable to the `pendingTransactions` array on the node with the help of the `addTransactionToPendingTransactions` method. Therefore, after the preceding line of code, add the following line:

```
bitcoin.addTransactionToPendingTransactions (newTransaction);
```

5. Now, broadcast the new transactions to all the other nodes inside the network. This can be done as follows:

```
bitcoin.netowrkNodes.forEach(networkNodeUrl => {
    //...
});
```

6. Inside this `forEach` loop, let's define the code to broadcast the transactions. To do this, make requests to the `/transaction` endpoints on all the other nodes inside the network. Therefore, define some options for these requests. Inside of the loop, let's add the following line:

```
const requestOptions = {

};
```

7. Then, define all our options, as shown here:

```
const requestOptions = {
    uri: networkNodeUrl + '/transaction',
    method: 'POST',
    body: newTransaction,
    json: true
};
```

8. Next, let's create an array of promises to push all the requests into that array, so that we can run all the requests at the same time. Let's define the array before the `forEach` loop as follows:

```
const requestPromises = [];
```

9. Then, after defining all of the options, make the request as follows:

```
requestPromises.push(rp(requestOptions));
```

With this preceding line of code, we're going to push all the requests into the `requestPromises` array. After the `forEach` loop has run, we should have all of the requests that we have defined inside the `requestPromises` array.

10. Next, let's run all of the requests. After the `forEach` loop, add the following line:

```
promise.all(requestPromises)
```

11. Finally, after all the requests have run, we'll add the following line:

```
.then(data => {

});
```

12. We're not actually going to use the data that comes back from all of these requests, but we are going to send a response, because, at this point, the entire broadcast is complete. Therefore, inside the preceding block of code, add the following highlighted code:

```
.then(data => {
    res.json({ note: 'Transaction created and broadcast
successfully.'})
});
```

By adding this preceding line of code, we have successfully completed building the `/transaction/broadcast` endpoint.

Refactoring the /transaction endpoint

We're going to refactor the `/transaction` endpoint in this section, so that it works perfectly with the new `/transaction/broadcast` endpoint. Let's apply the following steps to modify the endpoint:

1. To get started, go to the `dev/networkNode.js` file and delete everything that is in the `/transaction` endpoint. The only time the `/transaction` endpoint will be hit is when the broadcast takes place. When the `/transaction` endpoint is being hit, the `newTransaction` variable will be sent as data. This condition can be defined as follows:

```
app.post('/transaction', function(req, res) {
    const newTransaction = req.body;

};
```

In the preceding highlighted line, the `newTransaction` variable is sent to the `/transaction` endpoint with the help of `req.body`.

2. Next, add the new transaction to the `pendingTransactions` array of whichever node receives the call. To do this, the new `addTransactionToPendingTransactions` method will be used. Therefore, after the preceding line of code, add the following line:

```
bitcoin.addTransactionToPendingTransactions();
```

3. This method simply takes in the `newTransaction` variable that is received:

```
bitcoin.addTransactionToPendingTransactions(newTransaction);
```

4. Now, from the `addTransactionToPendingTransactions` method, we get the index of the block in which the transaction will be added. Let's save this block index in the new `/transaction` endpoint. At the start of the preceding line of code, add the variable as follows:

```
const blockIndex =
bitcoin.addTransactionToPendingTransactions(newTransaction);
```

5. The final thing to do is to send back a response. After the preceding line, add the following:

```
res.json({ note: 'Transaction will be added in block
${blockIndex}.'});
```

We've now finished refactoring the `/transaction` endpoint.

Testing the transaction endpoints

Let's test the `/transaction/broadcast` and `/transaction` endpoints to make sure that they are both working together correctly.

For this test, the first thing that we need to do is connect all the nodes together to make a network. You might remember how to do this, as we learned about it in Chapter 4, *Creating a Decentralized Blockchain Network*. We'll run through the steps quickly anyway, to refresh your memory.

Recapping how to create the network

Take a look at the following steps to understand how to connect all the nodes:

1. Go to Postman and hit the `/register-and-broadcast-node` route. This can be done on any of your nodes. In our example, let's use `localhost:3001`.
2. Now, inside the body, we want to add a new node to our network by passing its URL. Let's start with our second node. Take a look at the following screenshot:

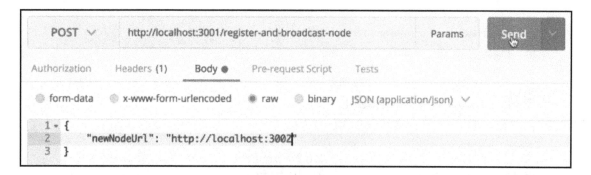

3. Then, click on the **Send** button to send the request. After sending the request, you'll receive a response that says **New node registered with the network successfully**. You can send all the remaining nodes in the same way.
4. To verify if all the nodes are connected properly to form a network, head over to the browser, type `localhost:3001/blockchain` in the address bar, and press *Enter*. You will see all the nodes in the `networkNodes` array.

Testing the transaction endpoints

Now that the blockchain network is set up, let's the test the endpoints that we created in the previous sections.

Let's create a transaction and send it to the `/transaction/broadcast` endpoint. Go back to Postman and hit the `/transaction/broadcast` endpoint at the node, which is hosted on port `3001`. Here, send some data as a transaction, as shown in the following screenshot:

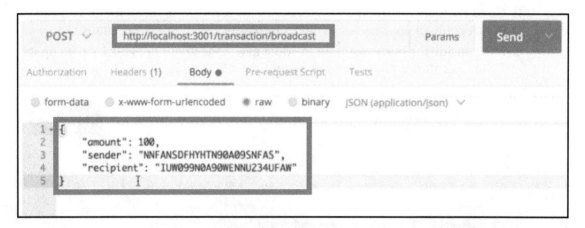

The transaction data that you're sending can be any random data. All we need is the amount, the sender, and the recipient. Once the transaction data is added, let's send this request by clicking on the **Send** button. If the transaction is sent successfully, a response will be received that says, **Transaction created and broadcast successfully**.

Now, go to the browser, and you should be able to see the transaction that we created on every single node of the network. Let's check whether this worked. In the address bar of the browser, type `localhost:3001/blockchain` and then press *Enter*. You should see the transaction data inside the `pendingTransactions` array, as shown in the following screenshot:

```
{
  "chain": [
    {
      "index": 1,
      "timestamp": 1524854646070,
      "transactions": [],
      "nonce": 100,
      "hash": "0",
      "previousBlockHash": "0"
    }
  ],
  "pendingTransactions": [
    {
      "amount": 100,
      "sender": "NNFANSDFHYHTN90A09SNFAS",
      "recipient": "IUW099N0A90WENNU234UFAW",
      "transactionId": "a8808e004a4b11e89d5087850f24d669"
    }
  ],
  "currentNodeUrl": "http://localhost:3001",
  "networkNodes": [
    "http://localhost:3002",
    "http://localhost:3003",
    "http://localhost:3004",
    "http://localhost:3005"
  ]
```

Here, the transaction that is inside the `pendingTransactions` array now also has a `transactionId` value, which starts with a random hash.

Next, open another tab and type `localhost:3002/blockchain` in the address bar, then press *Enter*. You can see that the same transaction data can be seen in the array:

If you go over to the other nodes in the network, you can carry out a similar check for all the remaining nodes. You can observe the same transaction data in the `pendingTransactions` array of each node. Every node inside the blockchain network is now aware that a new transaction was created.

You can try testing the endpoints with other transaction data as well. Try to change the amount to `500`, and the address of the sender and the recipient to a random hash string, and try sending this request to the node that's hosted on `localhost:3004`. This shouldn't make a difference, because the broadcast endpoint sends the transaction data to all the nodes inside of the network. Therefore, this request should work just like the last one. Checking the response on the browser, you should be able to see two transactions with different transaction IDs.

 Try experimenting with different transaction data to gain a clear understanding of how the `/transaction` and `/transaction/broadcast` endpoints work.

From the test, we can conclude that the `/transaction/broadcast` endpoint and the `/transaction` endpoint are both working properly as we expected them to.

In the next section, we'll continue synchronizing the network by refactoring the `/mine` endpoint, so that it will broadcast the new blocks that are created to the entire network.

Updating the mining information

The next thing that is required to synchronize the network is to update the `/mine` endpoint. We are also going to add a new endpoint, called `/receive-new-block`. There's a need to update the `/mine` endpoint so that whenever a new block is created by a node, that new block is broadcast to all the other nodes in the network. This means that every node on the network is aware that a new block has been created and all the nodes hosting the blockchain stay synchronized.

The updated mining process

Whenever a new block is mined, it will be mined on a particular node. To understand the updated mining process, let's assume that we want a node, hosted on port `3001`, to mine a new block for the blockchain:

1. Firstly, the `/mine` endpoint will be hit on the selected node. When the `/mine` endpoint is hit, a new block is created by doing a proof of work.

2. Once the new block is created, it is broadcast to all the other nodes in the network. All the other nodes will receive that new block at their `/receive-new-block` endpoint. This is shown in the following diagram:

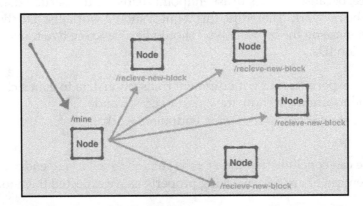

3. After the broadcast is complete, the entire network will be synchronized and all the nodes will host the same blockchain.

Another thing to note is that when a new block is broadcast and a node receives it, that new block will be added to the chain after the chain has validated that the block is legitimate. Then, the node clears out its `pendingTransactions` array, because all the pending transactions are now within the new block they just received.

In the next couple of sections, we're going to build this whole process step by step. As we build each of these steps, it should be easier to see how everything works together.

Refactoring the /mine endpoint

Let's refactor the `/mine` endpoint by implementing the following steps:

1. Head over to the `dev/networkNode.js` file. In the `/mine` endpoint, beneath the part where we had defined the `newBlock` variable, let's add the functionality to broadcast the new block to all the other nodes in the network. To do this, follow the same process that we introduced in the previous sections—that is, to loop through all the other nodes inside the network, make a request to the nodes, and send the `newBlock` variable as data:

```
bitcoin.networkNodes.forEach(networkNodeUrl => {

})
```

The preceding line mentions that for each of the `networkNodes`, we're going to make a request and send along the `newBlock`.

2. We then need some request options to send. These options will be defined as follows:

```
bitcoin.networkNodes.forEach(networkNodeUrl => {
    const requestOptions = {
    };

})
```

3. The first option in this object is the `uri`. The `uri` to which we want to send the request will be the `networkNodeUrl` and the new endpoint that we are going to create, which will be `/receive-new-block`. We'll work on this endpoint in the next section:

```
bitcoin.networkNodes.forEach(networkNodeUrl => {
    const requestOptions = {
        uri: networkNodeUrl + '/receive-new-block',
    };

})
```

4. The next option to be added is the method that will be used, which is the POST method:

```
bitcoin.networkNodes.forEach(networkNodeUrl => {
    const requestOptions = {
        uri: networkNodeUrl + '/receive-new-block',
        method: 'POST',
    };

})
```

5. Next, let's send along the data that will be inside the body. We also want to send along a `newBlock` instance:

```
bitcoin.networkNodes.forEach(networkNodeUrl => {
    const requestOptions = {
        uri: networkNodeUrl + '/receive-new-block',
        method: 'POST',
        body: { newBlock: newBlock }
    };

})
```

6. Finally, after the body, set `json` to `true`, as follows:

```
bitcoin.networkNodes.forEach(networkNodeUrl => {
    const requestOptions = {
        uri: networkNodeUrl + '/receive-new-block',
        method: 'POST',
        body: { newBlock: newBlock },
        json: true
    };

})
```

7. After that, make the request by adding the following highlighted line of code:

```
bitcoin.networkNodes.forEach(networkNodeUrl => {
    const requestOptions = {
        uri: networkNodeUrl + '/receive-new-block',
        method: 'POST',
        body: { newBlock: newBlock },
        json: true
    };
    rp(requestOptions)
})
```

8. Every time one of these requests is made, it's going to return a promise. Let's make an array of all of these promises by adding the following highlighted code:

```
const requestPromises = [];
bitcoin.networkNodes.forEach(networkNodeUrl => {
    const requestOptions = {
        uri: networkNodeUrl + '/receive-new-block',
        method: 'POST',
        body: { newBlock: newBlock },
        json: true
    };
    requestPromises.push(rp(requestOptions));
});
```

After our `forEach` loop has run, we should have an array that is filled with promises.

9. Next, let's run all of those promises. Therefore, after the `forEach` block, add the following code:

```
Promise.all(requestPromises)
.then(data => {
    // ....
})
```

After all of the requests have run, we want to carry out another calculation inside `.then(data => {     })`. If you remember, when a new transaction is created, the mining rewards transaction code, `bitcoin.createNewTransaction(12.5, "00" , nodeAddress);`, needs to be broadcast throughout the entire blockchain network. At the moment, when a new block is mined, we create a mining reward transaction, but it is not broadcast to the whole network. To broadcast it, the request will be sent to the `/transaction/broadcast` endpoint, because it already has the functionality to broadcast transactions. We're just going to make a call to this endpoint with the mining reward transaction data passed in.

10. Before passing the mining reward transaction data, however, we need some request options:

```
Promise.all(requestPromises)
.then(data => {
    const requestOptions = {
        uri: bitcoin.currentNodeUrl + '/transaction/broadcast',
        method: 'POST',
    };
})
```

11. The `body` data will be sent as an object. In the `body`, let's add the mining reward transaction data:

```
Promise.all(requestPromises)
.then(data => {
    const requestOptions = {
        uri: bitcoin.currentNodeUrl + '/transaction/broadcast',
        method: 'POST',
        body: {
            amount: 12.5,
            sender:"00",
            recipient: nodeAddress
        }
    };
})
```

12. Finally, after the `body`, set `json` to `true` by adding the following line:

```
json: true
```

13. Then, after the `requestOptions`, let's send the following request:

```
return rp(requestOptions);
```

At this point, inside the /mine endpoint, a bunch of calculations are being carried out to create a new block. Then, once the new block is created, it is broadcast to all the other nodes inside the network. After the broadcast is complete inside the .then block, a new request to the /transaction/broadcast endpoint is made. This request will create a mining reward transaction and the nodes will then broadcast it to the entire blockchain network. Then, after the request runs and all of the calculations are complete, a response is sent: **New block mined successfully.**

You can view the complete updated mine endpoint code at https:// github.com/PacktPublishing/Learn-Blockchain-Programming-with- JavaScript/blob/master/dev/networkNode.js.

Building the /receive-new-block endpoint

The next thing that we're going to do is build the /receive-new-block endpoint that we use in the updated /mine endpoint. Let's get started on building the endpoint:

1. In the dev/networkNode.js file, before the /register-and-broadcast-node endpoint, define the /receive-new-block endpoint as follows:

```
app.post('/receive-new-block', function(req, res) {
};
```

2. Inside this endpoint, the code expects to receive a new block that is being broadcast. Let's save that new block in a variable, as highlighted in the following code:

```
app.post('/receive-new-block', function(req, res) {
    const newBlock = req.body.newBlock;

};
```

3. When all of the other nodes receive this new block, they need to check whether it's actually a real block and whether it fits into the chain properly. To verify this, the previousBlockHash on the newBlock is checked to make sure that it's equal to the hash on the last block in the chain. For this, access to the last block in the chain is required:

```
app.post('/receive-new-block', function(req, res) {
    const newBlock = req.body.newBlock;
    const lastBlock = bitcoin.getLastBlock();
};
```

4. Next, let's test if the hash of the last block in the chain is equal to the `previousBlockHash` in the `newBlock` instance:

```
lastBlock.hash === newBlock.previousBlockHash;
```

5. This way, we know that this `newBlock` does indeed come right after the `lastBlock` in the chain. The preceding statement that is defined will return either `true` or `false`. The `true` or `false` value will be saved in a `correctHash` variable:

```
const correctHash = lastBlock.hash === newBlock.previousBlockHash;
```

6. After the preceding check, we also want to make sure that the `newBlock` has the correct index. This means that the `newBlock` should be one index above the `lastBlock` in the chain. Add the following check:

```
const correctIndex = lastBlock['index'] + 1 === newBlock['index'];
```

7. Next, two different actions need to be taken depending on whether or not the `newBlock` is legitimate. If the `newBlock` is legitimate, it should be accepted and added to the chain. If not, it should simply be rejected. In order to define this condition, let's use an `if-else` statement:

```
if (correctHash && correctIndex) {
    bitcoin.chain.push(newBlock);

}
```

8. Now, since the `newBlock` has been added to the chain, the `pendingTransactions` array needs to be cleared out, because the pending transactions are now inside the new block. Therefore, inside the `if` statement, the next condition to be added is as follows:

```
bitcoin.pendingTransaction = [];
```

9. Then, the final thing that needs to be done is to send a response back, saying that the block has been accepted and added to the chain. Inside the `if` statement, below the preceding line, add the response as follows:

```
res.json({
    note: 'New block received and accepted.',
    newBlock: newBlock
})
```

10. If the `newBlock` is not legitimate and does not pass either of the tests defined previously, then a response is sent inside of the `else` statement to indicate that the block was rejected:

```
else{
    res.json({
        note:'New block rejected.',
        newBlock: newBlock
    });
}
```

With the addition of this previous condition, we've finished building the `/receive-new-block` endpoint.

Testing the new and updated /mine endpoints

Let's test the updated /mine endpoint and the `/receive-new-block` endpoint that we just created. Basically, the /mine endpoint will mine the new block for us. It will also take that block and broadcast it across the entire blockchain network so that every node is synchronized and all the nodes have the same blocks and the same data. This is the result we expect to observe when we test the /mine endpoint:

1. To get started, you should have all five of the nodes running. You should also have connected them together to create a blockchain network.

2. Next, go to the browser. The first thing to do here is to choose a node to mine the new block. We have got five nodes to choose from but in our case, we will just stick with the first node. Therefore, type `localhost:3001/mine` in the address bar and then hit *Enter*. You will get an output like the following:

```
{
    "note": "New block mined & broadcast successfully",
    "block": {
        "index": 2,
        "timestamp": 1525033947030,
        "transactions": [],
        "nonce": 18140,
        "hash": "0000b9135b054d1131392c9eb9d03b0111d4b516824a03c35639e12858912100",
        "previousBlockHash": "0"
    }
}
```

It looks like the mine endpoint has worked perfectly. The response indicates that the new block has been mined and broadcast successfully. You can also see the new block in the preceding screenshot with its index.

3. Let's verify if the new block has been added to the network. First, verify it on the first node. In the browser, open another tab, type `localhost:3001/blockchain` in the address bar, and then press *Enter*. You can see that the new block has been added to the network as follows:

In the preceding screenshot, you might also notice that there are some transactions present in the `pendingTransactions` array. This pending transaction is actually the mining reward for the block that we just mined. The updated `/mine` endpoint defines that the mining reward transaction should be broadcast after a new block is created.

From now on, whenever a new block is created, the mining reward for that block will go into the `pendingTransactions` array and will be added to the next block. This is how mining rewards work in the Bitcoin blockchain. When we first created our blockchain in the first two chapters, we put the mining reward right into the block that we mined. Now that the blockchain is more advanced and we've got a decentralized network, it's important for us to follow best practices and put the mining reward into the next block.

Let's get back to the `/mine` endpoint and continue with the testing. Let's check the other nodes inside the network and verify whether the new block that was mined is added to those nodes or not. Also, let's check that the mining reward that was generated is also broadcast to the other nodes in the network.

Open another tab, type `localhost:3002/blockchain` in the address bar, and then press *Enter*. You will see the following output:

In the preceding screenshot, you can see that the node on port `3002` received the newly mined block, along with the mining reward transaction. You can verify this for the remaining nodes in the network.

Let's now mine another block from a different node. Instead of going to `localhost:3001`, type `localhost:3004/mine` in the browser's address bar, and then press *Enter*. The new block will be mined; the output will look as follows:

```
←  C  ⓘ localhost:3004/mine

▼ {
      "note": "New block mined & broadcast successfully",
    ▼ "block": {
          "index": 3,
          "timestamp": 1525034329263,
        ▼ "transactions": [
            ▼ {
                  "amount": 12.5,
                  "sender": "00",
                  "recipient": "9b96a8e04beb11e8ae4e9fbd43abb050",
                  "transactionId": "6e596ec04bec11e8ae4e9fbd43abb050"
              }
          ],
          "nonce": 47237,
          "hash": "0000349a9947bb85ca38786c6614567afb81a9269da0cb346b3532a8359f7da1",
          "previousBlockHash": "0000b9135b054d1131392c9eb9d03b0111d4b516824a03c35639e12858912100"
      }
  }
```

From the preceding screenshot, you can observe that this is the third block. This is correct because we have mined two blocks already. Inside the block's `transactions` array, you can see that we've got the mining reward from the previous block. This transaction was the mining reward that was generated when the node on port `3001` mined the previous block.

Let's go to `localhost:3001/blockchain` and verify if this new block that we just mined has been added to the network. You will see the following response:

In this screenshot, you can observe that the new block that was mined has been added to the node hosted on `3001`. The transaction array of this block consists of the mining reward from the previous block. We now also have a new mining reward in the `pendingTransactions` array, which was generated when the third block was mined. Following a similar process of verification, as we used before, you can check if the third block that we mined has been added to all the remaining nodes.

From these tests, it looks like the `/mine` endpoint is working just as it should. It's creating new blocks and broadcasting them to the entire network. This means the entire network is synchronized and has the exact same blockchain data, which is really important for a blockchain to work properly.

Let's test the endpoint a little further. Head over to Postman, create a couple of transactions, and then broadcast them. After that, let's mine a new block to see if the new transactions have been added to the blockchain correctly:

1. Go to your Postman now and create the following transaction:

```
{
    "amount": 100,
    "sender": "NNFANSDFHYHTN90A09SNFAS",
    "recipient": "IUW099N0A90WENNU234UFAW"
}
```

2. Next, in order to broadcast the transaction, hit the /transaction/broadcast endpoint. You can send this transaction data to any node and it should be broadcast to the entire network. In our example, let's send this transaction to the node on port 3002:

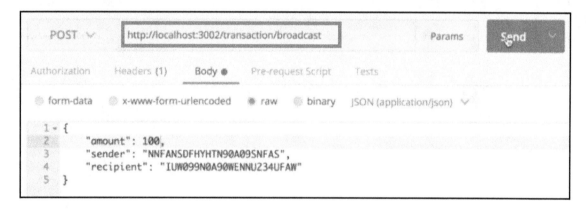

3. Now, click on the **Send** button. You'll then receive a response as the transaction was created and broadcast successfully.

   You can also try making other transactions just as we did previously, by changing the amount value and the sender's and recipient's addresses. Another test would be sending the transaction data to different nodes.

4. Let's now head back to the browser and check the nodes to verify that they've all received the transactions that we just created. As we loaded the node `3001` previously in our browser, let's refresh it. You should get the following output:

From the preceding screenshot, you can observe that the node has all three of the transactions that we created, plus it has the mining reward from the previous block inside the `pendingTransactions` array. Similarly, you can verify the `pendingTransaction` array for the remaining nodes. Thus, we can conclude that all of the transactions that we created are being broadcast to the entire network perfectly.

Now, let's mine a new block to verify whether all the pending transactions have been added to the new block. For this example, let's mine a new block on node `3003` by typing `localhost:3003/mine` in the address bar of the new tab. The response will indicate that the block was mined and broadcast successfully:

```
←   C   ⓘ localhost:3003/mine

   "block": {
      "index": 4,
      "timestamp": 1525034730445,
      "transactions": [
         {
               "amount": 12.5,
               "sender": "00",
               "recipient": "9e95df204beb11e8b3db516d48d8933b",
               "transactionId": "523271504bed11e8b3db516d48d8933b"
         },
         {
               "amount": 100,
               "sender": "NNFANSDFHYHTN90A09SNFAS",
               "recipient": "IUW099N0A90WENNU234UFAW",
               "transactionId": "e313fb304bed11e8a81ea7720ec623ec"
         },
         {
               "amount": 200,
               "sender": "NNFANSDFHYHTN90A09SNFAS",
               "recipient": "IUW099N0A90WENNU234UFAW",
               "transactionId": "f2a063904bed11e894050169f83c938a"
         },
         {
               "amount": 300,
               "sender": "NNFANSDFHYHTN90A09SNFAS",
               "recipient": "IUW099N0A90WENNU234UFAW",
               "transactionId": "fce309704bed11e8a81ea7720ec623ec"
         }
      ],
```

From the preceding screenshot, in the `transactions` array, it looks like all the transactions that we have created are present in the newly mined block. Let's go to all the nodes and verify whether the transactions that we created are added to the new block. On `localhost:3001`, you can observe the following output:

```
ⓘ localhost:3001/blockchain
, ,
{
    "index": 4,
    "timestamp": 1525034730445,
    "transactions": [
        {
            "amount": 12.5,
            "sender": "00",
            "recipient": "9e95df204beb11e8b3db516d48d8933b",
            "transactionId": "523271504bed11e8b3db516d48d8933b"
        },
        {
            "amount": 100,
            "sender": "NNFANSDFHYHTN90A09SNFAS",
            "recipient": "IUW099N0A90WENNU234UFAW",
            "transactionId": "e313fb304bed11e8a81ea7720ec623ec"
        },
        {
            "amount": 200,
            "sender": "NNFANSDFHYHTN90A09SNFAS",
            "recipient": "IUW099N0A90WENNU234UFAW",
            "transactionId": "f2a063904bed11e894050169f83c938a"
        },
        {
            "amount": 300,
            "sender": "NNFANSDFHYHTN90A09SNFAS",
            "recipient": "IUW099N0A90WENNU234UFAW",
            "transactionId": "fce309704bed11e8a81ea7720ec623ec"
        }
    ],
```

From this screenshot, we can observe that we've now got a fourth block that contains all the transactions that we sent. Then, if you check the `pendingTransactions` array, you can see that the transaction data has been cleared out and the new mining reward is present in it:

```
"pendingTransactions": [
    {
        "amount": 12.5,
        "sender": "00",
        "recipient": "9c68ed004beb11e8b1a28f078b897512",
        "transactionId": "4150e3c04bee11e8b1a28f078b897512"
    }
],
```

In this section, we created a couple of new transactions on different nodes. These were then broadcast to the whole network successfully. Then, we mined a new block and all the transactions we created were added to that new block successfully. On top of that, our newly mined block was broadcast to all the nodes inside our blockchain network. All of the nodes across our entire network are now synchronized and all contain the same blockchain data.

Summary

Up to now, you've achieved a lot in this book. You have created a decentralized blockchain network that's currently running across five nodes, and you built the functionality to synchronize the entire network, so that all the nodes have the exact same data. This mirrors how a blockchain would function in a real-world application.

In this chapter, we successfully synchronized the entire blockchain network by refactoring the endpoints to broadcast the data to all the nodes present in the network. We started by splitting the functionality of the `/createNewTransaction` method into two separate parts: the `/createNewTransaction` method and the `addTransactionToPendingTransactions` method. Then, we built the `/transaction/broadcast` endpoint to broadcast the newly created transaction to all the nodes in the network. We also refactored the `/transaction` endpoint, so that the `/transaction/broadcast` endpoint and the `/transaction` endpoint could work together. Later on in the chapter, we refactored the `/mine` endpoint and also built a new endpoint, `/receive-new-block`. With the help of these endpoints, the newly created blocks can be broadcast to all the nodes in the network.

In the next chapter, we'll be building consensus algorithms to make sure that all of the nodes inside our network can agree on the correct data to hold inside the blockchain.

6
Consensus Algorithms

In this chapter, we're going to build a consensus algorithm for the blockchain network. A consensus algorithm is a way for all of the nodes inside of the network to agree upon which data is correct and should be retained inside the blockchain. In order to build the consensus algorithm, we are first going to build a new method, called `chainIsValid`. This method will simply validate a blockchain by comparing all of the hashes of all of the blocks inside of the chain. After that, we are going to build a `/consensus` endpoint that we will hit whenever we want to use the consensus algorithm.

In this chapter, we're going to learn about the following:

- What the consensus algorithm is
- Building and testing the `chainIsValid` method
- Building and testing the `/consesnsus` endpoint

So, let's get started with the consensus algorithm.

What is the consensus algorithm ?

When a blockchain is built, it is running across hundreds or thousands of nodes, and every transaction and every block that's being created is broadcast to the entire blockchain network. There's a possibility that during these broadcasts a hiccup could occur, or maybe a certain node doesn't receive a piece of information or a transaction that took place.

There could even be a bad actor inside of the blockchain network, who is sending out false information or creating fraudulent transactions on their copy of a blockchain, and trying to broadcast them to the whole network to convince everybody that they are legitimate transactions. So, how do we solve this problem so that there are only legitimate blocks in the blockchain network?

This is where the consensus algorithm is going to help us out. The consensus algorithm will provide us with a way to compare one node to all the other nodes inside of the network to confirm that we have the correct data on that specific node. There are currently many different consensus algorithms out there being used for different blockchain networks. For our blockchain network, we're going to create a consensus algorithm that implements the *longest chain rule*.

Basically, the *longest chain rule* takes a look at a single node and the copy of the blockchain on that node, comparing the length of the chains on one node with the length of the chains on all the other nodes. During this comparison, if there is a chain found that has a longer length than the chain that's present on the chosen node, the algorithm is going to replace the chain that's on the chosen node with the longest chain in the network.

The theory behind using this is that we should be able to trust the longest chain to hold the correct data, because the most work was put into creating that chain. The longest chain has the most blocks in it and each of those blocks was mined by using a proof of work. Consequently, we can assume that the whole network contributed to the longest chain because of how much work went into that chain. For this reason, we're going to use a consensus algorithm that implements the longest chain rule. The Bitcoin blockchain network itself actually implements this longest chain rule in real life.

Building the chainIsValid method

Let's start building the consensus algorithm by creating a new method called `chainIsValid`. This method will validate whether or not a chain is legitimate. Let's get started with building this method:

1. In the `blockchain.js` file, after the `proofOfWork` method, let's define the method as follows:

```
Blockchain.prototype.chainIsValid = function() {

}
```

2. Now, this method will take in a `blockchain` as an argument, and will return to us whether the `blockchain` is valid or not:

```
Blockchain.prototype.chainIsValid = function(blockchain) {

}
```

We're going to use this `chainIsValid` method to validate the other chains inside of the network when we are comparing them to the chain that is hosted on the current node. In order to validate that the blockchain is legitimate, we're simply going to iterate through every block inside of the blockchain and verify whether or not all of the hashes align correctly.

You might recall from `Chapter 2`, *Building a Blockchain* that when the `createNewBlock` method was defined, that method consisted of the `previousBlockHash` and `hash` property. This `hash` property is the hash of the current block . To build the `chainIsValid` method, let's iterate through every block inside of the blockchain and make sure that the `previousBlockHash` property of a given block is exactly the same as the hash property in the previous block. Let's define this condition inside of the method as follows:

4. In order to iterate through every block inside of the blockchain, we'll use a `for` loop:

```
Blockchain.prototype.chainIsValid = function(blockchain) {
        for (var i = 1; i < blockchain.length; i++) {
        };

};
```

5. Inside of this `for` loop, let's compare the current block to the previous block:

```
Blockchain.prototype.chainIsValid = function(blockchain) {
        for (var i = 1; i < blockchain.length; i++) {
                const currentBlock = blockchain[i];
                const prevBlock = blockchain[i - 1];

        };

};
```

As we iterate through the entire chain on every iteration, the `currentBlock` will be the value of `i`, and the `prevBlock` will be the value of `i - 1`.

6. Next, all we want to do is compare the `previousBlockHash` property on the `currentBlock` with the hash property on the previous block. In order to do this, define the following condition in the method:

```
Blockchain.prototype.chainIsValid = function(blockchain) {
        for (var i = 1; i < blockchain.length; i++) {
                const currentBlock = blockchain[i];
                const prevBlock = blockchain[i - 1];
```

```
                    if (currentBlock['previousBlockHash'] !==
prevBlock['hash']) // chain is not valid...

        };

    };
```

When it comes to the preceding condition that we mentioned, if it is not satisfied, then we know that the chain is not valid, because the hashes are not lining up correctly.

7. To satisfy the verification condition, the previousBlockHash on the current block should be equal to the hash of the previous block. We're going to signify the aforementioned condition with the help of a flag inside of the method, as follows:

```
Blockchain.prototype.chainIsValid = function(blockchain) {
    let validChain = true;
    for (var i = 1; i < blockchain.length; i++) {
        const currentBlock = blockchain[i];
        const prevBlock = blockchain[i - 1];
        if (currentBlock['previousBlockHash'] !==
prevBlock['hash']) // chain is not valid...

        };

    };
```

Initially, we have the validChain variable reading equal to true. As we go through the blockchain and see that the hashes don't align properly, then we would want to set the validChain variable to false to signify that the chain is not valid.

8. Now let's get back to the if statement. Add the aforementioned condition to it:

```
Blockchain.prototype.chainIsValid = function(blockchain) {
    let validChain = true;
    for (var i = 1; i < blockchain.length; i++) {
        const currentBlock = blockchain[i];
        const prevBlock = blockchain[i - 1];
        if (currentBlock['previousBlockHash'] !==
prevBlock['hash']) validChain = false;

        };

    };
```

9. At the end of the loop, we can simply return a `validChain` variable and we'll get the value returned as `true` if the chain is valid, and `false` if it is not:

```
Blockchain.prototype.chainIsValid = function(blockchain) {
    let validChain = true;
    for (var i = 1; i < blockchain.length; i++) {
        const currentBlock = blockchain[i];
        const prevBlock = blockchain[i - 1];
        if (currentBlock['previousBlockHash'] !==
        prevBlock['hash']) validChain = false;

    };
    return validChain;
};
```

10. There is one more thing that we want to do, and that is to validate that every single block inside of the chain has the correct data. We can do this by rehashing the `currentBlock` by using the `hashBlock` method. If the generated hash starts with four zeros as we saw in Chapter 2, *Building a Blockchain*, then we know that all of the data is valid. However, if it does not start with the four zeros then we know the data inside of the block is definitely not valid.

All we're going to do is iterate through every block in the chain is to rehash every block and make sure that each hash starts with four zeros. So inside of the `for` loop let's mention this condition by first defining a variable as follows:

```
Blockchain.prototype.chainIsValid = function(blockchain) {
    let validChain = true;
    for (var i = 1; i < blockchain.length; i++) {
        const currentBlock = blockchain[i];
        const prevBlock = blockchain[i - 1];
        const blockHash = this.hashBlock ();
        if (currentBlock['previousBlockHash'] !==
        prevBlock['hash']) validChain = false;

    };
    return validChain;
};
```

11. The `hashblock()` method accepts parameters such as: `previousBlockhash`, `currentBlockData` and the `nonce`. Let's pass these parameters now:

```
const blockHash = this.hashBlock (prevBlock['hash']);
```

12. Next, we have to pass `currentBlockData` as parameter, which, as you might remember from the previous chapter, consists of the transactions in the `currentBlock` and the index of the `currentBlock`:

```
const blockHash = this.hashBlock(prevBlock['hash'], { transactions:
currentBlock['transactions'], index: currentBlock['index'] } );
```

13. Finally, the last parameter that we have to pass is `nonce`:

```
const blockHash = this.hashBlock (prevBlock['hash'], {
transactions: currentBlock['transactions'], index:
currentBlock['index'] } currentBlock['nonce']);
```

14. After defining these parameters, we should have the hash of `currentBlock` stored in the `blockHash` variable. Next, we just want to validate that the hash starts with the four zeros. So, inside of the `for` loop, we'll mention the following condition:

```
if (blockHash.substring(0, 4) !== '0000') validChain = false;
```

Now, we're basically iterating through the entire blockchain and simply checking two things:

- One check that we do is making sure that all of the hashes align properly. If they do not align properly, we indicate that the chain is not valid.
- The other check that we are doing is hashing every block, and making sure that the `blockHash` string starts with four zeros. If it does not start with the four zeros, then we indicate that the chain is not valid.

Now the `chainIsValid` method is just about done here. However, one important thing that you might have noticed is that we haven't checked the genesis block for any of the methods yet. In the loop that we defined in the preceding block of code, we're starting at position 1, and totally skipping position 0, which is the genesis block. The genesis block is a kind of special block, because we made it ourselves without doing a proof of work:

1. Consequently, in order to validate the genesis block, we just want to make sure that it has the properties that we initially put onto it. So, outside of the `for` loop, we'll mention this condition as follows:

```
const genesisBlock = blockchain[0];
```

2. Now we just want to check and verify that all of the properties on the genesis block are correct. If you remember in `Chapter 2`, *Building a Blockchain* where we defined the genesis block, we assigned to it values such as `nonce`, with a value of `100`, `previousBlockHash`, with a value `0`, and the `hash` of the string 0 as well. So, let's check for these properties now to make sure that they're correct. In the following snippet, we add the preceding line of code to the following variables:

```
const genesisBlock = blockchain[0];
const correctNonce = genesisBlock['nonce'] === 100;
const correctPreviousBlockHash = genesisBlock['previousBlockHash']
=== '0';
const correctHash = genesisBlock['hash'] === '0';
```

3. Finally, we want to verify that the genesis block should have no transactions in it. So, to check this, we'll mention the following condition:

```
const correctTransactions = genesisBlock['transactions'].length ===
0;
```

4. Now, if we do have a legitimate genesis block, then all of these variables that we defined should be the value true. If any of these variables are not valid, then we want to change the `validChain` variable to `false` so that we know the blockchain is not valid. Let's mention this condition as follows:

```
if (!correctNonce || !correctPreviousBlockHash || !correctHash ||
!correctTransactions) validChain = false;
```

Mentioning this last condition completes the `chainIsValid` method.

Testing the chainIsValid method

Now let's test the `chainIsValid` method by implementing the following steps:

1. In the `test.js` file, let's import the blockchain data structure and create a new instance of the blockchain, called `bitcoin`:

```
const Blockchain = require('./blockchain');
const bitcoin = new Blockchain();
```

2. Next, let's generate a blockchain for us to test. We'll do this by starting at one of the servers. So go to the terminal, type `npn run node_1` and press *Enter*. Then you'll receive the response, **Listening on port 3001**.

3. On node `3001`, now let's create a blockchain and add some data to it so that we can test the new blockchain. Currently, the blockchain on node `3001` only has the genesis block in it. So, let's add a couple more blocks to the chain by hitting the `/mine` endpoint. Therefore, in the browser, go to `localhost:3001/mine` to create a new block.

4. Now, if you go to `localhost:3001/blockchain`, you should be able to observe the new block as follows:

Thus, at node `3001`, we now have two blocks in the chain and one pending transaction, which is the mining reward transaction.

5. Next, let's create some transactions to add to the blockchain. To add the transaction, go to Postman and just add a couple of transactions there, as seen in the following screenshot. Let's send these transactions to `localhost:3001`, and also hit the `/transaction/broadcast` endpoint:

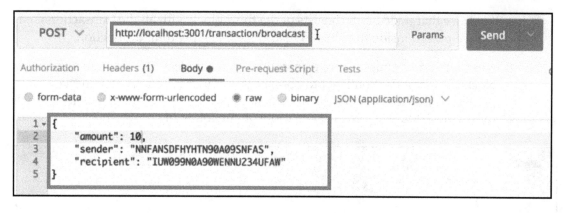

6. You can similarly add many other transactions to the node.

7. Once the transactions have been added, let's mine a new block by going to `localhost:3001/mine`. Once the new block has been mined, visit `localhost:3001/blockchain` in order to verify that the block has been added to the network. You should observe an output like the following:

```
{
    "index": 3,
    "timestamp": 1525295150900,
    "transactions": [
        {
            "amount": 12.5,
            "sender": "00",
            "recipient": "555dc5d04e4c11e89b44174d1b876bbf",
            "transactionId": "64b4c6504e4c11e89b44174d1b876bbf"
        },
        {
            "amount": 10,
            "sender": "NNFANSDFHYHTN90A09SNFAS",
            "recipient": "IUW099N0A90WENNU234UFAW",
            "transactionId": "881441704e4c11e89b44174d1b876bbf"
        },
        {
            "amount": 20,
            "sender": "NNFANSDFHYHTN90A09SNFAS",
            "recipient": "IUW099N0A90WENNU234UFAW",
            "transactionId": "8c835b604e4c11e89b44174d1b876bbf"
        },
        {
            "amount": 30,
            "sender": "NNFANSDFHYHTN90A09SNFAS",
```

You'll see that node 3001 consists of the third block with all the transaction data that we passed inside the block. We also have one pending transaction.

8. Next, let's add a couple more transactions to the node 3001 and then mine a new block on that node. You'll get to observe the similar output as seen in the previous case. The new transactions data that we added is now present inside the fourth block that we mined. Take a look at the following screenshot:

9. Next, let's mine two more blocks without any data in them. So now, we have a blockchain with six blocks in it. Out of these six blocks, two blocks don't have any transaction data present in them.

10. Copy the entire blockchain present on `localhost:3001` and paste it in the `test.js` file. Then, after pasting the data in the `test.js` file, let's save that pasted text as a variable:

```
const bc1 { //.... the entier blockchain that we copied and pasted
};
```

11. Let's use the `chainIsValid` method to validate the chain. To do this, in the `test.js` file, let's mention the following:

```
console.log('VALID:' , bitcoin.chainIsValid(bc1.chain));
```

12. Let's save the `test.js` file and run it.

Verifying the output of the test

Now, when we run this file, we should receive verification of a valid blockchain, because we didn't tamper with it and created it legitimately, using all of the correct methods. Let's verify whether or not the `chainIsValid` method works correctly:

1. Head over to the Terminal and cancel the previous processes that were running by typing ^C in the Terminal.

2. Once the processes are cancelled, then in the Terminal, let's type `node dev/test.js` and press *Enter*. As we haven't tampered with the blockchain, we'll get the `Valid: true` response, as seen in the following screenshot:

```
→ blockchain git:(master) ✗ node dev/test.js
VALID: true
```

Now, let's tamper with the blockchain a little bit and see if we can get a false value returned:

1. Inside of the blockchain data that we pasted into the `test.js` file, let's change one of the hashes on any one of the blocks to see if it invalidates the blockchain.

2. Once you have changed the hash of any block, save the file and run the test again. Since the data is tampered now, you'll get the `false` response:

```
➜  blockchain git:(master) ✗ node dev/test.js
VALID: false
```

Next, let's mess with some of the transaction data in one of the blocks. If we change any of the transaction data inside of one of the blocks, the chain should not be valid and we should receive a false response for the test.

Finally, let's test the genesis block, which is the first block in the chain:

```
  blockchain.js          test.js

1  const Blockchain = require('./blockchain');
2  const bitcoin = new Blockchain();
3
4
5  const bc1 = {
6  "chain": [
7  {
8  "index": 1,
9  "timestamp": 1525295039150,
10 "transactions": [],
11 "nonce": 100,
12 "hash": "0",
13 "previousBlockHash": "0"
14 },
15 {
16 "index": 2,
17 "timestamp": 1525295064849,
18 "transactions": [],
19 "nonce": 18140,
20 "hash": "0000b9135b054d1131392c9eb9d03b0111d4b51
21 "previousBlockHash": "0"
22 },
```

In the `test.js` file in the blockchain data that we pasted, let's change the `nonce` value to 10 from 100. After saving the file and running the test again in the Terminal, we should get the output returned as `false`. Since we tampered with the data in the blockchain in the `test.js` file, when we ran the test we got the response of `false`. This signifies that the blockchain is not valid or legitimate anymore, as the data inside it has been tampered with. So, from this test we can conclude that the `chainIsValid` method works perfectly, just as we expected it to.

A tiny modification to verify the results properly

Now, one tiny thing that we need to do to help us understand how the `chainIsValid` method works is to log out the `previousBlockHash` and the `currentBlock` hash of every single block so that we can compare them ourselves. Consequently, in the `chainIsValid` method inside of the `for` loop, let's add the following lines of code before the loop ends:

```
console.log('previousBlockHash =>', prevBlock [ 'hash']);
console.log('currentBlockHash =>', currentBlock [ 'hash']);
```

Let's save this modification and run the test again. This time, when we run the test, we should see all of the hashes logged out so that we can compare them for ourselves and see what's really happening inside of this method. After running the test, you should see the `previousBlockHash` and `currentBlockHash` values, as in the following screenshot:

```
➜  blockchain git:(master) ✗ node dev/test.js
previousBlockHash => 0
currentBlockHash  => 0000b9135b054d1131392c9eb9d03b0111d4b516824a03c35639e12858912100
previousBlockHash => 0000b9135b054d1131392c9eb9d03b0111d4b516824a03c35639e12858912100
currentBlockHash  => 0000c09685e31e57318e569b5fe3ca88ced727a29a0eb9cbea633e05056b4c29
previousBlockHash => 0000c09685e31e57318e569b5fe3ca88ced727a29a0eb9cbea633e05056b4c29
currentBlockHash  => 00001f3f4e1635cc930cdc41a954d19bcf457eeba8bf6c7be7aa4fe1489e64d3
previousBlockHash => 00001f3f4e1635cc930cdc41a954d19bcf457eeba8bf6c7be7aa4fe1489e64d3
currentBlockHash  => 000067295fb567842799b887910fe31cc8ca7544ec15a000b65005f6ac50df21
previousBlockHash => 000067295fb567842799b887910fe31cc8ca7544ec15a000b65005f6ac50df21
currentBlockHash  => 0000462c88b2814ebb930b13ac3c19dc698b2dca27b0c296e03f8a2ea104f74f
VALID:   true
```

From the preceding screenshot, you can observe that for every iteration, the `previousBlockHash` value matches the `currentBlockHash` value of the previous block. If you look at all of the hashes, you can see them logged out in pairs. From the screenshot, we can observe that we have many pairs of identical hashes, which is what makes the blockchain valid.

Building the /consensus endpoint

Now, let's build the /consensus endpoint, which will use the chainIsValid method that we built in the previous section. Carry out the following steps to build the endpoint:

1. Let's go to networkNode.js file and, after the /register-node-bulk endpoint, define the /consensus endpoint as follows:

```
app.get('/consensus', function(req, res) {

});
```

2. Next, inside of the /consensus endpoint, let's make a request to every other node inside of the blockchain network to get their copies of the blockchain and compare them to the copy of the blockchain that's hosted on the current node that we're currently on:

```
app.get('/consensus', function(req, res) {
    bitcoin.networkNodes.forEach(networkNodeUrl => {

    });

});
```

3. Inside of this forEach loop, let's do the same things that we've done countless times while defining the other endpoints in the previous chapters. So, the first thing we have to do for the requests is define some options as follows:

```
app.get('/consensus', function(req, res) {
    bitcoin.networkNodes.forEach(networkNodeUrl => {
        const requestOptions = {
            uri: networkNodeUrl + '/blockchain',
            method: 'GET',
            json: true
        }
    });

});
```

4. After defining the options, we need to request-promise the requestOptions and push all of these requests into a promise array because each of these requests returns a promise to us:

```
app.get('/consensus', function(req, res) {
    const requestPromises = [];
    bitcoin.networkNodes.forEach(networkNodeUrl => {
```

```
                        const requestOptions = {
                                uri: networkNodeUrl + '/blockchain',
                                method: 'GET',
                                json: true
                        }
                        requestPromises.push(rp(requestOptions));
                });

        });
```

5. Once the `forEach` loop has ran, we'll have an array that's filled up with all of the requests. Next, let's run the requests as follows:

```
app.get('/consensus', function(req, res) {
        const requestPromises = [];
        bitcoin.networkNodes.forEach(networkNodeUrl => {
                const requestOptions = {
                        uri: networkNodeUrl + '/blockchain',
                        method: 'GET',
                        json: true
                }
                requestPromises.push(rp(requestOptions));
        });
        Promise.all(requestPromises)
```

6. Then, let's use the data that we receive from all of these promises. This data that we're receiving is going to be an array of blockchains from every node inside of the network. So, after the preceding line of code, let's define the code as follows:

```
.then(blockchains => {

});
```

7. Now let's iterate through all of these `blockchains` that came from the other nodes inside of the network, and see if there is a blockchain inside of the other node that is longer than the copy of the blockchain hosted on the current node. We'll start by cycling through all of the blockchains that we got in the responses:

```
.then(blockchains => {
        blockchains.forEach(blockchain => {
                //....
        });
});
```

8. Basically, all we want to do inside of the `forEach` loop is identify whether one of the blockchains from the other nodes in the network is longer than the blockchain hosted on the current node. In order to do this, let's define a couple of variables to keep track of all of the data, as follows. The first variable that we want to define is the length of the blockchain hosted on the current node:

```
.then(blockchains => {
        const currentChainLength = bitcoin.chain.length;
        blockchains.forEach(blockchain => {
            //....
        });
});
```

9. Next, let's define a variable that will change if we come across a longer blockchain in the `blockchains` array. The first thing we want to define is the `maxChainLength` variable:

```
.then(blockchains => {
        const currentChainLength = bitcoin.chain.length;
        let maxChainLength = currentChainLength;
        blockchains.forEach(blockchain => {
            //....
        });
});
```

10. Next, we want to define a variable called `newLongestChain`. Initially we're going to set it as equal to null:

```
.then(blockchains => {
        const currentChainLength = bitcoin.chain.length;
        let maxChainLength = currentChainLength;
        let newLongestChain = null;
        blockchains.forEach(blockchain => {
            //....
        });
});
```

11. Then, the last variable that we'll define will be called `newPendingTransactions`. Let's set this as equal to `null` initially, as well:

```
.then(blockchains => {
        const currentChainLength = bitcoin.chain.length;
        let maxChainLength = currentChainLength;
        let newLongestChain = null;
        let newPendingTransactions = null;
        blockchains.forEach(blockchain => {
            //....
```

```
        });
    });
```

12. Now, inside the `forEach` loop, we're looking to see if there is a longer chain inside of the blockchain network than is currently on the node that we are on. If there is a longer chain inside the network, then change these aforementioned variables to reflect that. Consequently, inside of the `forEach` loop, define the `this` condition as follows:

```
.then(blockchains => {
        const currentChainLength = bitcoin.chain.length;
        let maxChainLength = currentChainLength;
        let newLongestChain = null;
        let newPendingTransactions = null;
        blockchains.forEach(blockchain => {
            if (blockchain.chain.length > maxChainLength) {
                maxChainLength = blockchain.chain.length;
                newLongestChain = blockchain.chain;
                newPendingTransactions =
                blockchain.pendingTransactions;
            };
        });
    });
```

Now, after the `forEach` loop has ran, we'll have all of the data required to determine if we need to replace the chain that is hosted on this current node. Next, after the loop, let's define the following conditions:

```
if (!newLongestChain || (newLongestChain &&
    !bitcoin.chainIsValid(newLongestChain)))
{
        res.json({
            note: 'Current chain has not been replaced.',
            chain: bitcoin.chain
        });
}
```

Basically, what we're stating in this `if` statement is that if there is no `newLongestChain` meaning, then the current chain is the longest. Alternatively, if there is a new longest chain but that new chain is not valid, then in these two cases we don't want to replace the blockchain that's hosted on the current node. So we're going to send back the note that says 'Current chain has not been replaced'.

Otherwise, if there is a `newLongestChain` and that chain is valid, now is when we want to replace the blockchain that's hosted on the current node with the longest chain in the network. We'll define all this inside of the else block as follows:

```
else {
        bitcoin.chain = newLongestChain;
        bitcoin.pendingTransactions = newPendingTransactions;
        res.json({
                note: 'This chain has been replaced.',
                chain: bitcoin.chain
        });
}
```

Quick review of the build process

The first thing that we did in this endpoint is made requests to all of the other nodes in the network so that we could access the blockchain that is hosted on each of them. After we ran all of these requests, we then had access to all of the blockchains that are hosted on all of the other nodes inside of the network. We then iterate through all of the other blockchains inside of the network with the help of the `forEach` loop. And as we iterated through the other blockchains, and if we find a longer chain we then update the `maxChainLength`, `newLongestChain`, and `newPendingTransactions` variables to reflect that. Then, when the `forEach` loop is complete, we'll know if there is a chain on the network longer than the blockchain hosted on the current node. If there is a longer chain found inside of the network, we'll have access to the `pendingTransactions` of that blockchain. So, after the `forEach` loop has ran, we'll then have access to all of the data necessary to replace the erroneous blockchain that's hosted on the current node.

We then state whether there is no new longer chain or if there is no chain longer than the blockchain hosted on the current node. If there is a longer chain inside of the network, but that chain is not valid, then in both of these cases we do not want to replace the blockchain that's hosted on the current node, so we simply send back a response that says the current chain has not been replaced.

On the other hand, if there is a longer chain inside of the network and that chain is valid, then we'll want to replace the blockchain that's hosted on the current node. We simply send back a response saying that this chain has been replaced, as well as sending back the new blockchain.

This is how the consensus algorithm and the `/consensus` endpoint will work.

Testing the /consensus endpoint

Let's test the consensus endpoint that we just built. So, what should this /consensus endpoint do? When we call the /consensus endpoint on a specific node, it should confirm for us that that particular node has the correct blockchain data in it, and the node is in sync with the rest of the network. Let's get started with building the test:

1. Our first step is to make a network that consists of the first four nodes. So let's go to Postman and hit the register-and-broadcast-node endpoint on the node that's hosted on 3001.

2. Let's add the second node to the network, as seen in the following screenshot. We'll then click on the **Send** button, receiving the response, **New node registered with network successfully**:

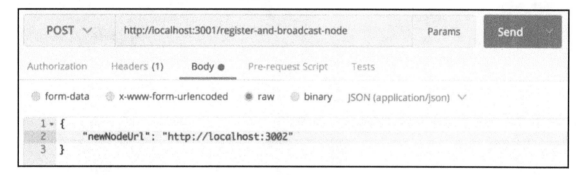

3. Similarly, you can register the remaining nodes, 3003 and 3004, to the network. Now, if you go to the browser and check all the nodes, you will observe that all the nodes from 3001 to 3004 are connected to each other, but node 3005 is not.

4. Next, what we want to do is mine a couple of blocks on the blockchain network, except for the fifth node. So in the browser, let's hit localhost: 3001/mine. This will mine one block for us on node 3001.

5. Similarly, let's mine two blocks on localhost:3003 and one block on localhost:3004. Now, all of these nodes should have five blocks in them. You verify this by hitting localhost:3001/blockchain in the browser. You will get to observe all five of the blocks that we just added.

6. At this point, we want to connect the fifth node to the blockchain network. So, let's go to Postman and send the request for 3005, as seen in the following screenshot:

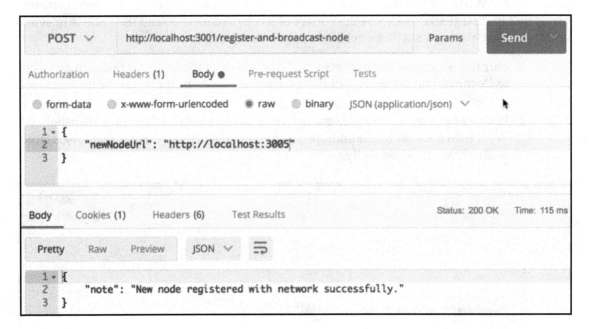

7. So now, node 3005 should be connected to the network. You can verify this in the browser as follows:

```
←  →  C  ⓘ localhost:3005/blockchain

▼ {
    ▼ "chain": [
        ▼ {
               "index": 1,
               "timestamp": 1525707050094,
               "transactions": [],
               "nonce": 100,
               "hash": "0",
               "previousBlockHash": "0"
          }
      ],
      "pendingTransactions": [],
      "currentNodeUrl": "http://localhost:3005",
    ▼ "networkNodes": [
          "http://localhost:3002",
          "http://localhost:3003",
          "http://localhost:3004",
          "http://localhost:3001"
      ]
  }
```

Now that 3005 is part of the network, this is where the problem arises: node 3005 does not have the correct blockchain data inside of the blockchain. It should have all of the five blocks that the other nodes have. This is where the /consensus endpoint comes into play. We should be able to hit the /consensus endpoint and resolve this issue. After we do this, we should expect the blockchain on node 3005 to have the same data as all the other nodes inside of the network.

Let's try this now. Open another tab in the browser, and in the address bar, type `localhost:3005/consensus` and then run it by pressing *Enter*. You should observe similar output to that seen in the following screenshot:

```
←  →  C  ①  localhost:3005/consensus

▼ {
      "note": "This chain has been replaced.",
   ▶  "chain": [ … ] // 5 items
  }
```

In the preceding screenshot, we get the response, **This chain has been replaced**, and the new blockchain data then replaces the old data on this node. Let's verify this node by going to another tab in the browser and hitting `localhost:3005/blockchain`. You'll see that all the blocks that were present in the network are added to the node on 3005. Thus the node on 3005 now has the correct blockchain data. We achieved this by hitting the /consensus endpoint on node 3005. Now, all of the nodes inside of the blockchain network should have exactly the same data.

Now, if you again try to hit the /consensus endpoint on the node on 3005, we would get the following response:

```
←  →  C  ①  localhost:3005/consensus

▼ {
      "note": "Current chain has not been replaced.",
   ▼  "chain": [
      ▼ {
             "index": 1,
             "timestamp": 1525707033090,
             "transactions": [],
             "nonce": 100,
             "hash": "0",
             "previousBlockHash": "0"
        },
      ▼ {
             "index": 2,
             "timestamp": 1525707566564,
             "transactions": [],
             "nonce": 18140,
             "hash": "0000b9135b054d1131392c9eb9d03b0111d4b516824a03c35639e12858912100",
             "previousBlockHash": "0"
        },
```

We received such a response because all the blocks that were present in the network were already added to node `3005` when we previously ran the consensus endpoint.

From this test, we can conclude that the `/consensus` works perfectly and as expected. The `/consensus` endpoint has the ability to correct a node inside of the blockchain if it has the wrong data.

It is recommended that you mess around with the `/consensus` endpoint and test it in different ways. Add some transactions to the data and make sure that it correctly resolves nodes that hold the wrong data. By testing this endpoint a little bit more, you will become more familiar with how it is works under the hood.

Summary

All blockchains have a consensus algorithm, and in this chapter, we built our own consensus algorithm that implements the longest chain rule. We started by building the `chainIsValid` method. In this method, we simply iterated through every single block inside of the blockchain, and compared hashes on every block to make sure that they are correct. Then we moved on to test the method. In addition to this, we built the `/consensus` endpoint with the help of the `chainIsValid` method.

In the next chapter, we're going to build a block explorer that we'll be able to access on the browser. This block explorer will allow us to interact with the blockchain through a user interface.

7
Block Explorer

In this chapter, let's build a block explorer that will allow us to interact with the blockchain. A block explorer is simply a user interface that will allow us to explore the data inside of the blockchain. It will allow us to search for a specific block, specific transaction, or specific address, and then display that particular information in a visually appealing format.

The first thing that we'll do to build the block explorer is to add some new methods and endpoints to the blockchain, in order to search for the data. Then, let's add a frontend to the block explorer, so we can use it in the browser.

In this chapter, we'll cover the following topics:

- What is a block explorer?
- Defining the block explorer endpoints
- Building the `getBlock`, `getTransaction`, and `getAddressData` methods
- Building and testing `/block/:blockHash`, `/transaction/:transactionId`, and `/address /:address` endpoints
- Developing our block explorer's interface and testing it.

So, let's get started on building our block explorer.

What is a block explorer?

A block explorer is an online platform that allows you to navigate through the blockchain, searching for various things including addresses, blocks, transactions, and so on. For example, if you visit `https://www.blockchain.com/explorer`, you can see a block explorer utility for the Bitcoin and Ethereum blockchains, as follows:

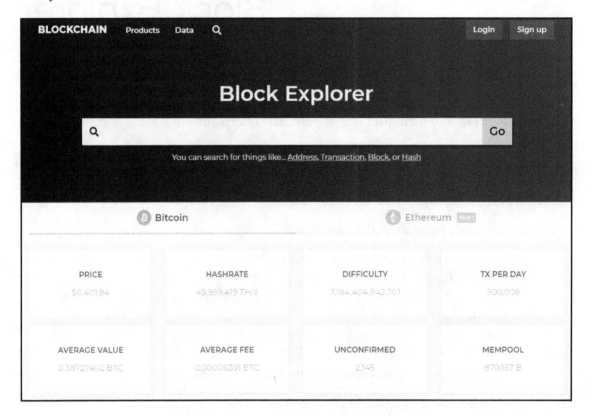

Inside of this block explorer, you can search the entire blockchain for a specific block, hash, or transaction, or any other piece of data that is required. The utility also displays results on an interface that's easy to understand. For example, if we search for `Block #549897` in the block explorer, you'll see all the details of that particular block, as seen in the following screenshot:

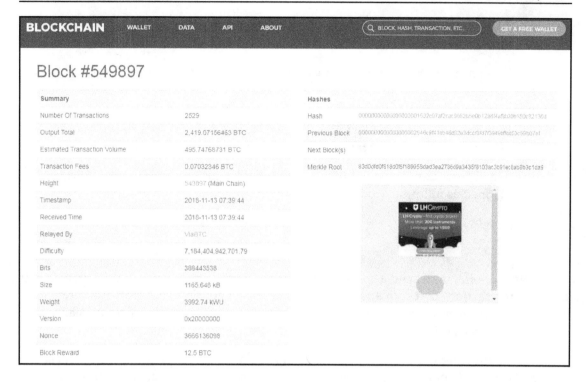

This is exactly what we're going to build for our blockchain in this chapter.

Defining the block explorer endpoints

In order for the block explorer to function correctly, we'll need to query the blockchain for addresses, block hashes, and transaction IDs so that we can search for a particular parameter and get that particular piece of data in return. Consequently, the first step that we'll need to carry out is to build a few more endpoints. To do this, lets proceed with the following steps:

1. Go to the `dev/networkNode.js` file and after the `/consensus` endpoint, let's define the first endpoint of our block explorer, `/block/:blockHash`, as follows:

   ```
   app.get('/block/:blockHash', function(req, res) {

   });
   ```

   A specific `blockHash` will be sent with this endpoint, which, as a result, will simply return to us the block that the input of `blockHash` corresponds to.

2. The next endpoint that we'll build will be `/transaction/:transactionId`. This is defined as follows:

```
app.get('/transaction/:transactionId', function(req, res) {

});
```

With this endpoint, send a `transactionId`, and in the response, we should expect to get the correct transaction that this ID corresponds to.

3. Finally, the third endpoint that we'll build is `/address/:address`, which is defined as follows:

```
app.get('/address/:address', function(req, res) {

});
```

With this endpoint, we'll send a specific address, and in response, you should expect to get all of the transactions that correspond to this address—every time this specific address has either sent or received Bitcoin—in response. you'll also get to know the current balance of this address, which is how many Bitcoins this address currently owns.

So, these are the three endpoints that you'll be building in this chapter. For each of these endpoints, we will build a specific method in the blockchain data structure that will query the blockchain for the correct piece of data. So, let's create methods that query the blockchain for a specific block hash, transaction, and address.

Building the getBlock method

Let's build a new method called `getBlock` that will take the given `blockHash` and search the entire blockchain for the block associated with that particular hash. In order to build the `getBlock` method, follow these steps:

1. Go to the `dev/blockchain.js` file and after the `chainIsValid` method, define this new method as follows:

```
Blockchain.prototype.getBlock = function(blockHash) {

};
```

2. Inside this method, we want to iterate through the entire blockchain and search for the block that has a particular `blockHash` value. Then, this method will return that specific block to us. We're going to do all this with the help of a `for` loop:

```
Blockchain.prototype.getBlock = function(blockHash) {
    this.chain.forEach(block => {
    });
};
```

When defining the `for` loop, we cycle through every single `block` in the blockchain.

3. Next, inside the loop, mention the conditions with the help of `if` statements, as follows:

```
Blockchain.prototype.getBlock = function(blockHash) {
    this.chain.forEach(block => {
            if (block.hash === blockHash)
    });
};
```

4. To signify that the correct block that we're searching for is found, we're going to use a flag. Let's define this flag variable as has been highlighted in the following code:

```
Blockchain.prototype.getBlock = function(blockHash) {
    let correctBlock = null;
    this.chain.forEach(block => {
            if (block.hash === blockHash)
    });
};
```

5. As we iterate through all of the blocks in the chain, if we come across the correct block, we assign it to `correctBlock`. Let's mention this condition as follows:

```
Blockchain.prototype.getBlock = function(blockHash) {
    let correctBlock = null;
    this.chain.forEach(block => {
            if (block.hash === blockHash) correctBlock = block;
    });
};
```

6. Finally, at the end of this method, we want to return the `correctBlock` as follows:

```
Blockchain.prototype.getBlock = function(blockHash) {
    let correctBlock = null;
    this.chain.forEach(block => {
            if (block.hash === blockHash) correctBlock = block;
    });
    return correctBlock
};
```

Building the /block/:blockHash endpoint

Let's use the `getBlock` method inside of `/block/:blockHash` endpoint to retrieve a specific block by its `blockHash`. Let's follow these next steps to build the endpoint:

1. The first thing that we want to do in this endpoint is to use the `blockHash` value that is sent with the `/block/:blockHash` request. We can access this `blockHash` on the `req.params` object. Go to the `dev/networkNode.js` file and in the `/block/:blockHash` endpoint that we defined previously, add the following highlighted code:

```
app.get('/block/:blockHash', function(req, res) {
        const blockHash = req.params.blockHash;
});
```

Essentially, when we hit the `/block/:blockHash` endpoint, we're accessing the hash value of a block present on a particular node in the network. We're also accessing the hash value using the `req.params` object, which will give us access to any value in the `/block/:blockHash` URL that has a colon in front of it. Consequently, when a user makes a request to this endpoint, they're going to send in a `blockHash` in the URL, and then we can grab that `blockHash` with the help of `req.params.blockHash`. We're then going to save that value inside the `blockHash` variable.

2. Next, inside the endpoint, we want to use the `getBlock` method that we created in the previous section. We'll add that method to the endpoint, as highlighted in the following code:

```
app.get('/block/:blockHash', function(req, res) {
        const blockHash = req.params.blockHash;
        const correctBlock = bitcoin.getBlock(blockHash);
});
```

By this point in the code, the block that we're looking for should be present in the `correctBlock` variable.

3. Finally, send back the `correctBlock` variable as a response, so let's add the following highlighted code to the endpoint:

```
app.get('/block/:blockHash', function(req, res) {
        const blockHash = req.params.blockHash;
        const correctBlock = bitcoin.getBlock(blockHash);
        res.json({
                block: correctBlock
        });
});
```

This is how we build the `/block/:blockHash` endpoint using the `getBlock` method. Now, let's test this endpoint and verify whether or not it's working properly.

Testing the /block/:blockHash endpoint

In order to test the `/block/:blockHash` endpoint, follow these steps:

1. Let's first check how many blocks are present in the blockchain. Go to the browser and type `localhost:3001/blockchain` in the address bar and then press *Enter*. You'll see the single genesis block present inside of the blockchain, as follows:

2. You need to add a couple more blocks to this chain. To do this, go over to another tab in the browser, type `localhost:3001/mine`, and then press *Enter*. Using the same process, let's generate one more block. We should now have three blocks inside the chain: one genesis block and the two blocks we just added.

3. In order to test the `/block/:blockHash` endpoint, let's simply take the hash value of one of these blocks and use it to test the endpoint. Let's copy the hash value of the third block in the chain, as in the following screenshot:

```
{
    "index": 3,
    "timestamp": 1525719679166,
    "transactions": [
        {
            "amount": 12.5,
            "sender": "00",
            "recipient": "e1bdc540522811e8b8260ba3c0b9d501",
            "transactionId": "047344c0522911e8b8260ba3c0b9d501"
        }
    ],
    "nonce": 50265,
    "hash": "00002641f1f7825aa670db5ee632036d80a507edcdd35124c66700dd4fc99dc6",
    "previousBlockHash": "0000b9135b054d1131392c9eb9d03b0111d4b516824a03c35639e12858912100"
}
```

4. Next, go to another tab in the browser. Type `localhost:3001/block` in the address bar and then paste the hash value that we copied directly after this URL. Take a look at the following screenshot for a better understanding:

5. Now, we know that the hash that we've used is present in the third block in the chain. So, we should expect to get the third block returned to us as a result of running the `/block/:blockHash` endpoint. Now press *Enter* and the correct block should be returned to us as output:

From the preceding screenshot, we can observe that the correct block is returned to us. The returned block consists of the hash value that we used in the `/block/:blockHash` endpoint to search for the block.

In a similar manner, you can now try searching for another block from the chain using the endpoint and the hash value of that particular block.

Now, if we were to send in the wrong hash or a hash that doesn't exist with the endpoint, then we should expect to get **null** returned to us as output, instead of the block being returned. Let's try this by sending the wrong hash value to the `/block/:blockHash` endpoint. In the address bar of the browser, type `localhost:3001/block`, then add a fake hash value to it and press *Enter*. The following output should be returned:

From the preceding screenshot, you can observe that `block` is equal to `null`. This means that the hash value used to search the block doesn't exist in the chain. Consequently, from the test, we can conclude that the `/block/:blockHash` endpoint works perfectly and as expected.

Defining the getTransaction method

Let's add a new method on the blockchain data structure called `getTransaction`. This will allow us to get a specific transaction by passing `transactionId`. We'll use this new method inside of the `/transaction/:transactionId` endpoint. So, let's get started!

1. Go to the `dev/blockchain.js` file, and after the `getBlock` method, define the `getTransaction` as follows:

```
Blockchain.prototype.getTransaction = function(transactionId) {

});
```

This method is very similar to the `getBlock` method. Here, we'll iterate through the entire chain and will set a flag equal to the correct transaction that we are looking for.

2. The next step in building this method will be to iterate through the entire blockchain. For this, use the `forEach` loop as follows:

```
Blockchain.prototype.getTransaction = function(transactionId) {
    this.chain.forEach(block => {
    });

});
```

3. Since, in this method, we're looking for transactions, we need to iterate through every single transaction on every block in the chain. Therefore, we need to add another `for` loop inside the preceding `for` loop:

```
Blockchain.prototype.getTransaction = function(transactionId) {
    this.chain.forEach(block => {
        block.transactions.forEach(transaction => {
        });
    });

});
```

4. Now that we have access to every single transaction on the blockchain, we simply need to compare the `transactionId` of every transaction with the `transactionId` that we're looking for. When the two match, then we know we have found the correct transaction. Let's define this condition inside the loop as follows:

```
Blockchain.prototype.getTransaction = function(transactionId) {
      this.chain.forEach(block => {
            block.transactions.forEach(transaction => {
                  if (transaction.transactionId ===
transactionId) {
                        };
            });
      });

});
```

5. Next, just like we did inside of the `getBlock` method, we want to set a flag to indicate that we have found the correct transaction inside the `getTransaction` method. Consequently, at the top of both of the loops, define the flag variable and use it as follows:

```
Blockchain.prototype.getTransaction = function(transactionId) {
      let correctTransaction = null;
      this.chain.forEach(block => {
            block.transactions.forEach(transaction => {
                  if (transaction.transactionId ===
transactionId) {
                              correctTransaction = transaction;
                        };
            });
      });

});
```

6. Now, just to make this method a little bit more useful, we're also going to send back the block in which we found the transaction we were hunting for. To do this, define another flag as follows:

```
let correctBlock = null;
```

7. If we then find the transaction we're looking for, set the condition as follows:

```
Blockchain.prototype.getTransaction = function(transactionId) {
      let correctTransaction = null;
      let correctBlock = null;
      this.chain.forEach(block => {
            block.transactions.forEach(transaction => {
                  if (transaction.transactionId ===
transactionId) {
                              correctTransaction = transaction;
                              correctBlock = block;
                        };
```

```
                                });
                        });

        });
```

8. And then, finally, the last thing to do is to return both variables as output. Let's define this return condition as follows, outside of both the loops:

```
return {
        transaction: correctTransaction,
        block: correctBlock
};
```

Building the /transaction/:transactionId endpoint

Let's build the /transaction/:transactionId endpoint by using the getTransaction method that we built in the previous section. Let's begin:

1. The first thing to do inside of this endpoint is to store the transaction ID sent as a request parameter. Let's store that in a transactionId variable, as follows:

```
app.get('/transaction/:transactionId', function(req, res) {
        const transactionId = req.params.transactionId;
});
```

2. The next thing to do is use the getTransaction method inside of the endpoint. To do this, add the following to the preceding code:

```
app.get('/transaction/:transactionId', function(req, res) {
        const transactionId = req.params.transactionId;
        bitcoin.getTransaction(transactionId);
});
```

3. From the getTransaction method, we get an object returned to us that has the transaction we're looking for, and the block that the transaction is in. We want to store this data in a variable called transactionData, as follows:

```
app.get('/transaction/:transactionId', function(req, res) {
        const transactionId = req.params.transactionId;
        const trasactionData =
bitcoin.getTransaction(transactionId);
});
```

4. Finally, we want to send back a simple response with the `transactionData` variable in it:

```
app.get('/transaction/:transactionId', function(req, res) {
        const transactionId = req.params.transactionId;
        const trasactionData =
bitcoin.getTransaction(transactionId);
        res.json({
    transaction: trasactionData.transaction,
    block: trasactionData.block
        });

});
```

And this is how we build the `/transaction/:transactionId` endpoint.

Testing the /transaction/:transactionId endpoint

Now, it's time to test the `/transaction/:transactionId` endpoint to verify that it works as expected. However, before doing that, we need to add some transaction data and blocks to the blockchain.

Adding new transactions and blocks to the blockchain

Similar to what we did in the previous section, first, let's add some transactions and blocks to the blockchain:

1. Therefore, head over to Postman and hit the `localhost:3001/transaction/broadcast` endpoint to send the transaction to all the nodes in the network.
2. Now, send a couple of example transactions to the network. You can create the transactions as seen in the following screenshot:

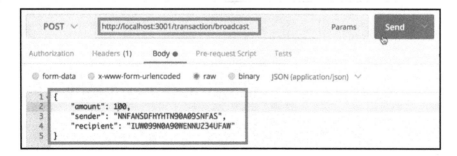

3. After adding the transaction data, click on the **Send** button to send the transaction to the network. Similarly, you can add one more transaction of `"amount": 200` and send that to the network.

4. Next, mine a new block so that we can add these transactions into the blockchain. In the browser, open a tab and type `localhost:3001/mine` into the address bar. The new block will then be created:

```
{
    "note": "New block mined & broadcast successfully",
    "block": {
        "index": 2,
        "timestamp": 1525722213503,
        "transactions": [
            {
                "amount": 100,
                "sender": "NNFANSDFHYHTN90A09SNFAS",
                "recipient": "IUW099N0A90WENNU234UFAW",
                "transactionId": "d1870460522e11e8a46723bdd5d30502"
            },
            {
                "amount": 200,
                "sender": "NNFANSDFHYHTN90A09SNFAS",
                "recipient": "IUW099N0A90WENNU234UFAW",
                "transactionId": "d7623170522e11e8a46723bdd5d30502"
            }
        ],
        "nonce": 119336,
        "hash": "0000ccfe439cc66d21d95802a6e35685cfe1ea6e7b27b8cd7ee67a5d4cbf1bd9",
        "previousBlockHash": "0"
    }
}
```

5. Next, send another transaction of `"amount"`: 300 and send this to the network using the previously mentioned process. Once the transaction has been sent, let's mine a block again to add the transaction to the blockchain:

```
{
    "note": "New block mined & broadcast successfully",
    "block": {
        "index": 3,
        "timestamp": 1525722243100,
        "transactions": [
            {
                "amount": 12.5,
                "sender": "00",
                "recipient": "b39c0540522e11e8a46723bdd5d30502",
                "transactionId": "ed226e30522e11e8a46723bdd5d30502"
            },
            {
                "amount": 300,
                "sender": "NNFANSDFHYHTN90A09SNFAS",
                "recipient": "IUW099N0A90WENNU234UFAW",
                "transactionId": "faa15350522e11e8a46723bdd5d30502"
            }
        ],
        "nonce": 16333,
        "hash": "00001708da724bff4de08fd4a158802f3183141ec91db70ba5fced51fdd1aa3b",
        "previousBlockHash": "0000ccfe439cc66d21d95802a6e35685cfe1ea6e7b27b8cd7ee67a5d4cbf1bd9"
    }
}
```

6. Now, add two more transactions, with `"amount"`: values of 400 and 500, and send those to the network. Lastly, mine a block again to add the transactions that we created now to the blockchain:

```
localhost:3001/blockchain    x    localhost:3001/mine    x

←  →  C  ① localhost:3001/mine

{
    "note": "New block mined & broadcast successfully",
    "block": {
        "index": 4,
        "timestamp": 1525722271949,
        "transactions": [
            {
                "amount": 12.5,
                "sender": "00",
                "recipient": "b39c0540522e11e8a46723bdd5d30502",
                "transactionId": "fec47020522e11e8a46723bdd5d30502"
            },
            {
                "amount": 400,
                "sender": "NNFANSDFHYHTN90A09SNFAS",
                "recipient": "IUW099N0A90WENNU234UFAW",
                "transactionId": "06a11280522f11e8a46723bdd5d30502"
            },
            {
                "amount": 500,
                "sender": "NNFANSDFHYHTN90A09SNFAS",
                "recipient": "IUW099N0A90WENNU234UFAW",
                "transactionId": "0975dd60522f11e8a46723bdd5d30502"
            }
```

Now, if you go to `localhost:3001/blockchain`, you'll see all of the blocks and transactions that we just added to the blockchain.

Testing the endpoint

After adding transactions and blocks to the blockchain, let's test the `/transaction/:transactionId` endpoint:

1. Go to the browser and open another tab. In the address bar,
   type `localhost:3001/transaction/` and then append a `transactionId`
   value from any block present in the blockchain to the end of this URL and press
   Enter. Take a look at the following screenshot for reference:

2. Once you run this endpoint, the following output should be returned:

```
← → C  ⓘ localhost:3001/transaction/faa15350522e11e8a46723bdd5d30502

{
    "transaction": {
        "amount": 300,
        "sender": "NNFANSDFHYHTN90A09SNFAS",
        "recipient": "IUW099N0A90WENNU234UFAW",
        "transactionId": "faa15350522e11e8a46723bdd5d30502"
    },
    "block": {
        "index": 3,
        "timestamp": 1525722243100,
        "transactions": [
            {
                "amount": 12.5,
                "sender": "00",
                "recipient": "b39c0540522e11e8a46723bdd5d30502",
                "transactionId": "ed226e30522e11e8a46723bdd5d30502"
            },
            {
                "amount": 300,
                "sender": "NNFANSDFHYHTN90A09SNFAS",
                "recipient": "IUW099N0A90WENNU234UFAW",
                "transactionId": "faa15350522e11e8a46723bdd5d30502"
            }
```

In the preceding screenshot, you can observe that we had the transaction, associated with the `transactionId` that we passed with endpoint, returned as output. We also had the block returned, which consisted of the particular `transactionId` that we were looking for.

3. Now, carry out another example with a `transactionId` which doesn't exist in the blockchain. To do this, go to the browser and type `localhost:3001/transaction/` into the address bar. After doing this, add a random hash value to the endpoint. Take a look at the following screenshot:

4. When you run this endpoint you will get the value null returned as output, as seen in the following screenshot:

```
{
    "transaction": null,
    "block": null
}
```

The null value returned as seen in the preceding screenshot, indicates to us that this `transactionId` does not exist in the blockchain.

From the test, we can conclude that the `/transaction/:transactionId` endpoint and the `getTransaction` method are working just as they should.

Building the getAddressData method

We'll build a new method on the blockchain prototype, called `getAddressData`, and we'll use this method inside of the `/address/:address` endpoint to fetch the data for a specific address that we are searching for:

1. Let's build this new method inside of the `blockchain.js` file. After the `getTransaction` method, define the `getAddressData` method as follows:

```
Blockchain.prototype.getAddressData = function(address) {

});
```

2. Now, the first thing that we want to do inside of this method is to get all of the transactions that are associated with the address and put them into a single array. Let's define that array now:

```
Blockchain.prototype.getAddressData = function(address) {
        const addressTransactions = [];
});
```

3. Then, we want to cycle through all of the transactions inside of the blockchain. If any of those blocks have the address we're searching for as the recipient or sender in a transaction, then we want to add all those transactions into the `addressTransactions` array. Let's define this condition as follows. The first step is cycling through all of the blocks on the blockchain:

```
Blockchain.prototype.getAddressData = function(address) {
        const addressTransactions = [];
        this.chain.forEach(block => {
        });
});
```

4. Now, in order to access the transactions that are inside the blockchain, we need to cycle through all of the transactions that are present on each block. So, inside of the `forEach` loop, we will have to define another `forEach` loop as follows:

```
Blockchain.prototype.getAddressData = function(address) {
        const addressTransactions = [];
        this.chain.forEach(block => {
                block.transactions.forEach(transaction => {
                });
        });
});
```

5. Now, inside of the `forEach` loop that we defined just now, we have access to every single transaction that is on the blockchain. We just want to test each transaction to see if the sender or the recipient address matches with the address that we're searching for:

```
Blockchain.prototype.getAddressData = function(address) {
        const addressTransactions = [];
        this.chain.forEach(block => {
                block.transactions.forEach(transaction => {
                        if(transaction.sender === address ||
                            transaction.recipient === address) {
                          addressTransactions.push(transaction);
                        }
                });
        });
});
```

At this point in the code, we are cycling through all of the transactions inside of our blockchain. If we come across a transaction in which the sender address or the recipient address equals the address we are looking for, then we push that transaction into the `addressTransactions` array. So, after both `forEach` loop has completed, we'll have an array that has all of the transactions associated with the address that we're are searching for inside of the array.

Knowing the balance

The next thing that we want to do is to cycle through the `addressTransactions` array to figure out what the balance of the address that we are searching for is. In order to know the balance:

1. Let's first define a variable `balance` as follows:

```
let balance = 0;
```

2. Next, we want to cycle through all of the transactions inside of the `addressTransactions` array. We will do that with the help of the `forEach` loop as follows:

```
let balance = 0;
addressTransactions.forEach(transaction => {

});
```

3. Inside the loop, mention the conditions with the help of `if` and `else-if` statements, as follows:

```
let balance = 0;
addressTransactions.forEach(transaction => {
        if (transaction.recipient === address) balance +=
transaction.amount;
          else if (transaction.sender === address) balance -=
transaction.amount;
});
```

4. Finally, at the end of the `forEach` loop, we want to return an object that has a property of `addressTransactions` that matches our `addressTransactions` array, and the same match for `addressBalance`:

```
let balance = 0;
addressTransactions.forEach(transaction => {
        if (transaction.recipient === address) balance +=
transaction.amount;
          else if (transaction.sender === address) balance -=
transaction.amount;
});
return {
        addressTransactions: addressTransactions,
        addressBalance: balance
};
```

And with that, we're done building the `getAddressData` method.

Developing the /address/:address endpoint

Now, let's build the `/address/:address` endpoint and we'll use the `getAddressData` method inside of this endpoint. The `/address/:address` endpoint will be very similar to the `/block/:blockHash` and `/transaction/:transactionId` endpoints, so you shouldn't find it too challenging:

1. The first thing that we want to do inside of the endpoint is to store the address in a variable:

```
app.get('/address/:address', function(req, res) {
        const address = req.params.address;
});
```

2. The next thing that we want to do is use the `getAddressData` method to get all of the data for the given address. In order to do that, we will add the following highlighted code to the endpoint:

```
app.get('/address/:address', function(req, res) {
        const address = req.params.address;
        bitcoin.getAddressData(address);
});
```

3. From this method, we get an object returned to us that has the `addressTransactions` and the `addressBalance` in it. We want to store this data in a variable as follows:

```
app.get('/address/:address', function(req, res) {
        const address = req.params.address;
        const addressData = bitcoin.getAddressData(address);
});
```

4. Then, finally, we want to return the response that contains this data as follows:

```
app.get('/address/:address', function(req, res) {
        const address = req.params.address;
        const addressData = bitcoin.getAddressData(address);
        res.json({
                addressData: addressData
        });

});
```

This is how we build the `/address/:address` endpoint. Now, let's test this endpoint to check that it's working well.

Testing the /address/:address endpoint

In order to test the endpoint, we need to add some transaction data to the blockchain, let's follow these steps to do that:

1. Go to the browser and explore the blockchain that's present on `localhost:3001`. You'll observe that there's only one block present here. So, let's add more transaction data and blocks to it.

2. To do this, go to Postman and send the transaction data to
`localhost:3001/transaction/broadcast`. While creating these transactions,
we want to make sure that we keep track of a specific address so that we can
check for it when we test the `/address/:address` endpoint. In order to keep
track of this specific address, let's change the first three letters of one of the
addresses to JEN.

3. Let's create the first transaction. Set the `"amount":` value to `100`, and add JEN to
the sender's address for this transaction:

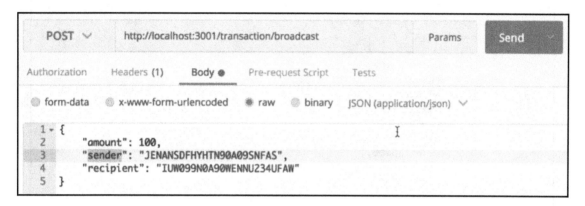

4. Then, click on **Send** to send the transaction to node `3001`. Then, on similar lines,
make another transaction for `amount: 200` and this time, add JEN to the
recipient's address, and keep the sender's address as a random hash:

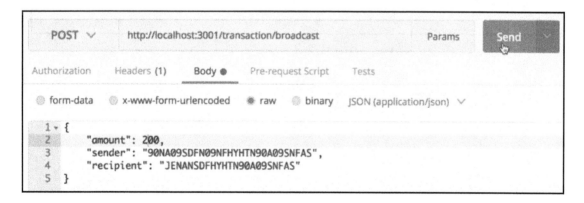

5. Now, mine a block to add these transactions to the blockchain. Go to `localhost:3001/mine` and mine a new block in the chain as follows:

```
{
    "note": "New block mined & broadcast successfully",
    "block": {
        "index": 2,
        "timestamp": 1525725550989,
        "transactions": [
            {
                "amount": 100,
                "sender": "JENANSDFHYHTN90A09SNFAS",
                "recipient": "IUW099N0A90WENNU234UFAW",
                "transactionId": "92d00ca0523611e8a3e385ffad54bee1"
            },
            {
                "amount": 200,
                "sender": "90NA09SDFN09NFHYHTN90A09SNFAS",
                "recipient": "JENANSDFHYHTN90A09SNFAS",
                "transactionId": "a8c56320523611e8a3e385ffad54bee1"
            }
        ],
        "nonce": 187272,
        "hash": "0000f154b445ef2b4ed78d522441adb59b1921b765b8ac49427de507c2997516",
        "previousBlockHash": "0"
    }
}
```

Similarly, you can make a couple more transactions by changing the amount value and interchanging the sender's and recipient's addresses, with `JEN` present in the address. Once a few transactions are created, mine a block to add these new transactions to the blockchain. Then, create new transactions again, and give them different amounts by interchanging the sender's and recipient's addresses. Again, mine a new block to add the transactions to the blockchain.

You can then explore the whole blockchain, with the new transactions and blocks that we added to it, by going to `localhost:3001/blockchain`. You'll be presented with a bunch of blocks and transactions inside the blockchain.

Now, in order to test the `/address/:address` endpoint, let's follow these steps:

1. Head over to the browser, and hit the `localhost:3001/address/` endpoint in a new tab.
2. Then, copy one of the addresses from the transactions that we just added to the blockchain and paste it in the endpoint. Take a look at the following screenshot for reference:

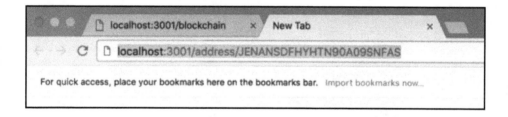

3. Now, when we run this endpoint, we should see all the transactions associated with that particular address, along with the Bitcoin balance of that particular address. Take a look at the following screenshot:

In the preceding screenshot, we get the `addressData` property returned, which consists of the `addressTransactions` array and the `addressBalance` property. The `addressTransactions` array consists of all the transactions associated with the address that we mentioned in the endpoint. In addition, the `addressBalance` property consists of the balance of Bitcoins of the address that we mentioned in the endpoint:

4. Next, you can try to check the balance of the node address by copying the recipient's address of the mining reward transactions and pasting it in the `/address/:address` endpoint, as we did for the previous example.

5. After running this endpoint, you'll see the balance of mining reward transactions. Try implementing many other similar examples to get a clear understanding of how the `/address/:address` endpoint works.

6. Another example you can try to implement is to pass an address that doesn't exist in the blockchain. You will get the following response returned:

From the preceding screenshot, we can observe that the `addressTransactions` array is empty, as there are no transactions associated with the nonexistent address that we had as input. Furthermore, the `addressBalance` value for the nonexistent address is `0`. Consequently, we can conclude from the test that the `/address/:address` endpoint is working just as it should.

Adding the block explorer file

Let's understand how to set up the block explorer frontend. The block explorer will be a user interface with which we can interact with the blockchain from the browser. In order to build this user interface and make it functional, we need to use HTML, CSS, and JavaScript.

Now, instead of building all of the frontend by yourself, you can find an entire prebuilt frontend at the following link: `https://github.com/PacktPublishing/Learn-Blockchain-Programming-with-JavaScript/blob/master/dev/block-explorer/index.html`. We're not building the entire frontend in this section, because that's not the focus of this book.

To build the frontend, all you have to do is copy the file from the link provided and add that to the project's file structure. Now, go to the `dev` folder and create a new folder inside it, called `block-explorer`. Inside this `block-explorer` folder, create a file called `index.html`, into which you need to paste the supplied code for the frontend and then save the file. You'll get a quick overview of what this frontend code consists of and how the code functions in the next section.

Building the /block-explorer endpoint

Let's build an endpoint that will retrieve the `block-explorer` file for us:

1. Go to the `dev/networkNode.js` file, and in here, create a new endpoint that will send this file to us. Define the endpoint as follows:

```
app.get('/block-explorer', function(req, res) {

});
```

2. Now, inside of this endpoint, all we want to do is send back the `index.html` file to whoever called this endpoint:

```
app.get('/block-explorer', function(req, res) {
    res.sendFile('./block-explorer/index.html', { root: __dirname
});
});
```

You must have observed in the previous sections that we usually use res.json, which is a way to send JSON data. However, in this endpoint, we want to send the whole file, so we'll use the res.sendFile method instead. Note that in the preceding code, we used { root: __dirname }. This code term indicates that we should look into the directory in which the project is stored, and search in there for the file with the /block-explorer/index.html path. This is why we added this option to the endpoint as a second parameter, and this is how we build an endpoint to send the index.html file.

3. Next, save the networkNode.js file and verify whether this endpoint works by hitting localhost:3001/block-explorer in the browser. You will then be presented with the block explorer frontend, as follows:

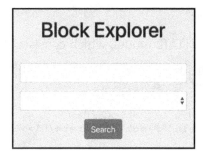

Everything that you see here in this frontend is contained within the index.html file that we just created.

Block explorer file explanation

In this section, we're simply going to walk through the index.html file that we created in the previous section. We'll do this to gain a better understanding of what is going on. So, let's get started.

Inside the index.html file, we have all of the HTML and JavaScript code to give the necessary functionality to the block explorer. This code also allows us to hit the API, and lastly, we just have some CSS and styles, which make everything look nice in the browser.

The code begins by importing a couple of libraries, such as angular.js, to hit the API, along with jQuery, Bootstrap, and some Bootstrap styles to make everything functional and aesthetically pleasing:

```
<head>
  <title>Block Explorer</title>
  <script
src="https://ajax.googleapis.com/ajax/libs/angularjs/1.5.6/angular.min.js">
</script>
  <script src="https://code.jquery.com/jquery-3.3.1.min.js"
integrity="sha256-FgpCb/KJQlLNfOu91ta32o/NMZxltwRo8QtmkMRdAu8="
crossorigin="anonymous"></script>
  <script
src="https://maxcdn.bootstrapcdn.com/bootstrap/3.3.7/js/bootstrap.min.js"
integrity="sha384-
Tc5IQib027qvyjSMfHjOMaLkfuWVxZxUPnCJA712mCWNIpG9mGCD8wGNIcPD7Txa"
crossorigin="anonymous"></script>
  <link rel="stylesheet" type="text/css"
href="https://maxcdn.bootstrapcdn.com/bootstrap/4.0.0/css/bootstrap.min.css
">
</head>
```

Next, we have the body of the HTML model, which consists of the block explorer title:

```
<body ng-app="BlockExplorer">
  <div class="container" ng-controller="MainController">
    <div class="row">
      <div class="col-md-8 offset-md-2">
        <h1 id="page-title">Block Explorer</h1>
      </div>
    </div
```

Then, we have a text input form:

```
<div class="row">
    <div class="col-md-6 offset-md-3">
      <form ng-submit="search(searchValue)">
        <div class="form-group">
          <input type="text" class="form-control" ng-model="searchValue">
        </div>
```

Next, we have a select input with three options in it: Block Hash, Transaction ID, and Address:

```
<div class="form-group">
        <select class="form-control" ng-model="searchType">
                <option value="block">Block Hash</option>
                <option value="transaction">Transaction ID</option>
```

```
            <option value="address">Address</option>
        </select>
    </div>
```

To use this page, let's enter either a **Block Hash**, **Transaction ID**, or **Address** into the text field, and then select which one we're looking for from the drop-down menu, as seen in the following screenshot:

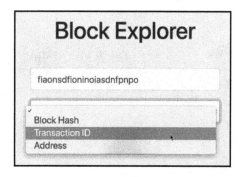

Lastly, in the HTML code, we just have some tables that will display all of our data for us once we have some data from the blockchain.

Furthermore, we also have some JavaScript code in our `index.html` file. In this JavaScript code, we use Angular to make the calls to our API:

```
window.app = angular.module('BlockExplorer', []);
app.controller('MainController', function($scope, $http) {
        $scope.block = null;
        $scope.transaction = null;
        $scope.addressData = null;
        $scope.initialSearchMade = false;
```

Then we have a method where we hit the `/block/:blockHash` endpoint whenever we select the **Block Hash** option:

```
$scope.fetchBlock = function(blockHash) {
        $http.get(`/block/${blockHash}`)
        .then(response => {
          $scope.block = response.data.block;
          $scope.transaction = null;
          $scope.addressData = null;
        });
    };
```

Similarly, we have the method for the `/transaction/:transactionId` endpoint:

```
$scope.fetchTransaction = function(transactionId) {
        $http.get(`/transaction/${transactionId}`)
        .then(response => {
          $scope.transaction = response.data.transaction;
          $scope.block = null;
          $scope.addressData = null;
        });
      };
```

We also have the method for the `/address/:address` endpoint:

```
$scope.fetchAddressData = function(address) {
        $http.get(`/address/${address}`)
        .then(response => {
          $scope.addressData = response.data.addressData;
          if (!$scope.addressData.addressTransactions.length) $scope
            .addressData = null;
          $scope.block = null;
          $scope.transaction = null;
        });
      };
```

Throughout the rest of this JavaScript, we just have a little bit more functionality and then we have the CSS styles towards the end of the code. Consequently, this code is contained in the `index.html` file. If you want to dig a little bit deeper into this to gain a clearer understanding, feel free to do so. You can also customize it however you would like to.

Then you press **Search**, and if the specified data exists in the blockchain, a table will be displayed that will show all of that data. If the data doesn't exist on our blockchain, you will get the result that no data was found. This is how the block explorer frontend will work.

At this point, we have built an entire block explorer frontend, and we have the backend of the block explorer—the three endpoints that we just created—in order to search through the entire blockchain.

In the next section, we're going to test the block explorer to make sure that it works perfectly.

Testing our block explorer

In this section, we're going to test the block explorer to make sure that it works correctly, and also to make sure that all endpoints and methods that we created in the previous chapter also work correctly. If the block explorer works, then we already know that the entire blockchain is also working correctly and is running on the decentralized blockchain network, so everything is wrapping up nicely now as we enter the final section of this chapter. Consequently, this is the last test that we will be doing. Let's follow these steps now to test the block explorer:

1. In order to test the block explorer, we should ensure that we have all five of the nodes running.

2. Next, head over to the browser and open up the block explorer by going to `localhost:3003/block-explorer`. You can actually go to a block explorer that's hosted on any of the nodes in the network, because the blockchain is hosted across the entire network.

3. Now, in order to test the block explorer, we need to add some data to the blockchain. To add data to the blockchain, we're just going to create a lot of transactions and create some new blocks similar to what we did in the previous sections. You can refer back to the previous chapters for a quick review on how to add transactions and blocks to the blockchain.

4. After adding the data, we can now test the block explorer. Let's first get a block by searching for its block hash. Let's select the **Block Hash** option:

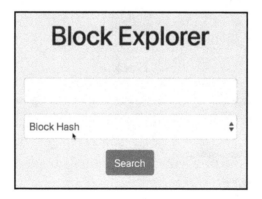

5. Then, from the blockchain, copy the hash value from any of the blocks and paste it into the block explorer:

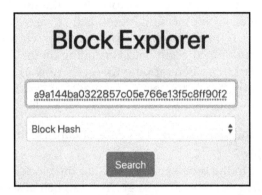

6. Now, click on the **Search** button. You should see a similar output as in the following screenshot:

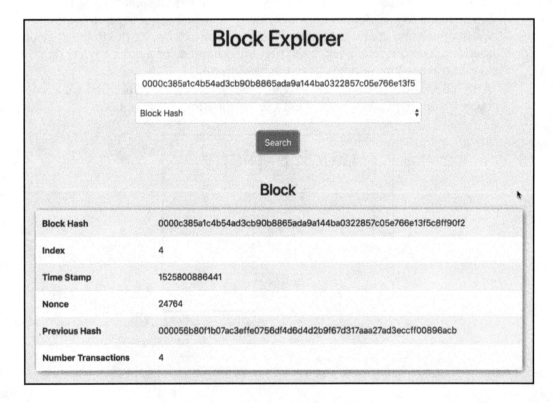

This is basically how the block explorer works. We enter a hash or a piece of data that we're looking for, and in return, we get that piece of data as output. From the preceding screenshot, we can observe that we had the block returned with an index of 4 for the hash value that we input to the block explorer. We also got all of the details related to that block. Furthermore, as you can probably tell for this search, we're hitting the `/block/:blockHash` endpoint.

7. Next, search for a transaction by inputting the `transactionId`. Go to block explorer and select the **Transaction ID** option. Then, go to the blockchain and copy a `transactionId` value from any block and input it to the block explorer:

8. Then click on the **Search** button. You'll see a similar output to the following:

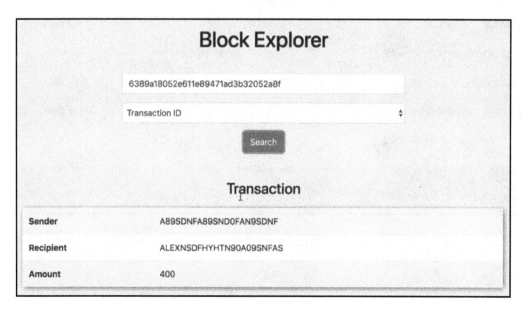

From the preceding screenshot, we can see that we got all of the transaction details related to the `transactionId` that we input to the block explorer. We also got to observe the balance amount of **400** bitcoins for that particular `transactionId`.

9. Finally, test the address endpoint. To do this, select the **Address** option from the block explorer and then input either the sender's or recipient's address from any of the blocks. Then click on the **Search** button. You should see the following output on the screen:

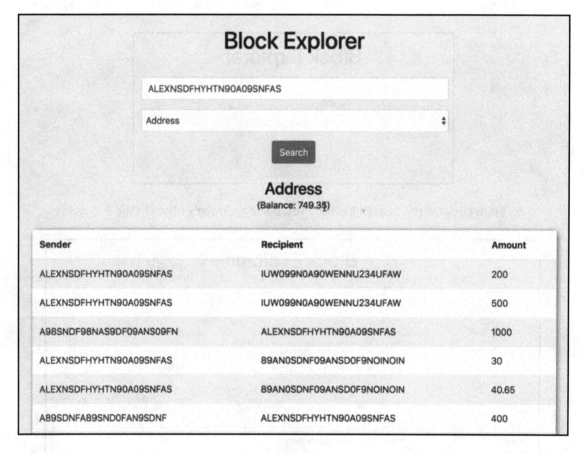

From the preceding screenshot, we can see that the address has a balance of **749.35** Bitcoins and we can see all of the transactions that are associated with the address that we've input.

Now, for any of these searches, if we input a piece of data that doesn't exist, we'll get the result back as follows:

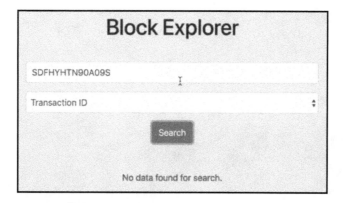

This proves that the block explorer works just as it should.

Summary

In this chapter, we built an amazing user interface to explore the blockchain that we have built in this book so far. We started by defining the necessary endpoints for querying the required data. Then we built methods such as `getBlock`, `getTransaction`, and `getAddressData` to help the endpoints to query the data. Furthermore, we developed the `/block/:blockHash`, `/transaction/:transactionId`, and `/address/:address` endpoints. After doing this, we added the block explorer's frontend code to our blockchain directory and then tested the block explorer and all the endpoints that we developed.

With this chapter, we have reached the end of this book. By this point, we have built our very own blockchain and added all the necessary functionalities to it. In addition to this, we have also built our decentralized network and an interface to explore the blockchain.

The next chapter will be a quick summary of what we have learned throughout this book. We'll then explore what else we can do with the blockchain that we've developed.

In conclusion...

8

Welcome to the final chapter of the book. By now, you will have gained an in-depth knowledge of blockchain functions and how they are built. You must be getting excited to build your very own blockchain and explore its various functionalities!

Before we conclude this book, let's have a quick review of what we've learned so far and explore what improvements or amendments we can make to our blockchain to make it more secure and reliable.

So, let's get ready to take the last steps...

A quick review

With the completion of the previous chapter, we are done building our blockchain. If you think about how much you have accomplished throughout the entirety of this book, it's pretty impressive.

We started with nothing, and from there, we built a blockchain data structure, followed by an API to interact with it. We then turned our API into a decentralized blockchain network, and synchronized the data across the entire network running on multiple different nodes.

We then created a **consensus** algorithm to make sure that the data on all of our nodes was synchronized and legitimate. Finally, we built a block explorer to explore our blockchain through a user interface. Throughout this entire book, we have built a lot of functionalities, as well as an awesome blockchain prototype.

One important thing that you must be aware of is that, throughout this book, we have been running all five of our nodes on one computer.

However, if you were to download this entire project onto multiple different computers, you would be able to run each node on a separate computer to really simulate how a decentralized blockchain network works.

You would just have to make sure that every computer running your project is on the same network. Instead of having a localhost address, you would just have the IP address that each node is running on.

Try experimenting with this idea. It's pretty cool to see your blockchain network running across multiple different computers.

Areas of improvement

Now, there are a few areas where the blockchain could be improved. One of those areas is in error handling. Throughout this book, we didn't do much error handling, because we were focusing on getting the actual functionalities to work correctly, but to improve this blockchain we would definitely want to do a lot of error handling. This would ensure that our blockchain can't be hacked, and also make sure that it runs correctly.

Another area where this blockchain could be improved is when we are making transactions. Right now, when we make transactions, we send a certain amount of Bitcoin from one person to another, but at no point do we validate that the sender actually has this bitcoin to send.

One exercise we would encourage you to do is to go to our `createTransaction` method in our blockchain data structure, and then find a way to verify that the sender actually has the amount of Bitcoin to send. This would be a good practice project for you to try on your own. You would have to get the current balance of bitcoin that the sender has, and do a check to validate that they have enough Bitcoin to send in the transaction.

Another way that this blockchain could be improved is by making it into a decentralized application platform similar to Etherium. You would do this simply by adding a functionality to the blockchain that would allow you to store more data inside of each block, allowing you to store different types of data inside of each block, instead of just transactions. For example, you could store user data, administrative data, or any other type of data inside of each block. You would then use that data when you are generating the hash for each block, just like we use the transactions when we are generating the hashes.

There are a lot of ways that you can customize and improve on the blockchain we've built; however, right now, we have a fully functioning prototype blockchain that can be hosted on a decentralized blockchain network.

So, that's it from us. We hope you enjoyed this book, learned a lot, and had fun building the blockchain that we created!

Other Books You May Enjoy

If you enjoyed this book, you may be interested in these other books by Packt:

Learn Bitcoin and Blockchain
Kirankalyan Kulkarni

ISBN: 9781789536133

- Understand the concept of decentralization, its impact, its relationship with blockchain technology and its pros and cons
- Learn blockchain and bitcoin architectures and security
- Explore bitcoin and blockchain security
- Implement blockchain technology and its features commercially
- Understand why consensus protocols are critical in blockchain
- Get a grip on the future of blockchain

Building Enterprise JavaScript Applications
Daniel Li

ISBN: 9781788477321

- Practice Test-Driven Development (TDD) throughout the entire book
- Use Cucumber, Mocha and Selenium to write E2E, integration, unit and UI tests
- Build stateless APIs using Express and Elasticsearch
- Document your API using OpenAPI and Swagger
- Build and bundle front-end applications using React, Redux and Webpack
- Containerize services using Docker
- Deploying scalable microservices using Kubernetes

Leave a review - let other readers know what you think

Please share your thoughts on this book with others by leaving a review on the site that you bought it from. If you purchased the book from Amazon, please leave us an honest review on this book's Amazon page. This is vital so that other potential readers can see and use your unbiased opinion to make purchasing decisions, we can understand what our customers think about our products, and our authors can see your feedback on the title that they have worked with Packt to create. It will only take a few minutes of your time, but is valuable to other potential customers, our authors, and Packt. Thank you!

Index

P

Postman
  about 69
  installing 67, 68, 69, 71, 72, 73, 74, 75
Proof of Work (PoW) method
  about 49, 50, 51
  creating 51, 53
  testing 54, 55, 56, 57

prototype object 18, 19, 20, 21

S

SHA256 hashing function 43, 45

U

updated /mine endpoints
  testing 162, 164, 166, 167, 170, 171
updated mining process 155, 156

www.ingramcontent.com/pod-product-compliance
Lightning Source LLC
Chambersburg PA
CBHW080637060326
40690CB00021B/4963